SIR PERCEVAL OF GALLES

and

YWAIN AND GAWAIN

Chrétien de Troyes

The Thornton Manuscript
Lincoln Cathedral MS 91 (Thornton, c. 1440)

I

Here Begynnes the Romance of
Sir Percyvell of Galles

Lef, lythes to me
Two wordes or thre,
Of one that was faire and fre
   And felle in his fighte.
His righte name was Percyvell,
He was fosterde in the felle,
He dranke water of the welle,
   And yitt was he wyghte.
His fadir was a noble man;
Fro the tyme that he began,
Miche wirchippe he wan
   When he was made knyghte
In Kyng Arthures haulle.
Beste byluffede of alle,
Percyvell thay gan hym calle,
   Whoso redis ryghte.

Who that righte can rede,
He was doughty of dede,
A styffe body on a stede
   Wapynes to welde;
Tharefore Kyng Arthoure
Dide hym mekill honoure:
He gaffe hym his syster Acheflour,
   To have and to holde
Fro thethyn till his lyves ende,
With brode londes to spende,

3

For he the knyght wele kende.
He bytaughte hir to welde,
With grete gyftes to fulfill;
He gaffe his sister hym till
To the knyght, at ther bothers will,
With robes in folde.

He gaffe hym robes in folde,
Brode londes in wolde,
Mony mobles untolde,
His syster to take.
To the kirke the knyghte yode
For to wedde that frely fode,
For the gyftes that ware gude
And for hir ownn sake.
Sythen, withowtten any bade,
A grete brydale thay made,
For hir sake that hym hade
Chosen to hir make;
And after, withowtten any lett,
A grete justyng ther was sett;
Of all the kempes that he mett
Wolde he none forsake.

Wolde he none forsake,
The Rede Knyghte ne the Blake,
Ne none that wolde to hym take
With schafte ne with schelde;
He dose als a noble knyghte,
Wele haldes that he highte;
Faste preves he his myghte:
Deres hym none elde.

Sexty schaftes, I say,
Sir Percyvell brake that ilke day,
And ever that riche lady lay
   One walle and byhelde.
Thofe the Rede Knyghte hade sworne,
Oute of his sadill is he borne
And almoste his lyfe forlorne,
   And lygges in the felde.

There he lygges in the felde -
Many men one hym byhelde -
Thurgh his armour and his schelde
   Stoneyde that tyde.
That arghede all that ther ware,
Bothe the lesse and the mare,
That noble Percyvell so wele dare
   Syche dynttys habyde.
Was ther nowthir more ne lasse
Of all those that ther was
That durste mete hym one the grasse,
   Agaynes hym to ryde.
Thay gaffe Sir Percyvell the gree:
Beste worthy was he;
And hamewardes than rode he,
   And blythe was his bryde.

And thofe the bryde blythe be
That Percyvell hase wone the gree,
Yete the Rede Knyghte es he
   Hurte of his honde;
And therfore gyffes he a gyfte
That if he ever covere myghte

Owthir by day or by nyghte,
   In felde for to stonde,
That he scholde qwyte hym that dynt
That he of his handes hynte;
Sall never this travell be tynt,
   Ne tolde in the londe
That Percyvell in the felde
Schulde hym schende thus undire schelde,
Bot he scholde agayne it yelde,
   If that he were leveande.

Now than are thay leveande bathe;
Was noghte the Rede Knyghte so rathe
For to wayte hym with skathe.
   Er ther the harmes felle,
Ne befelle ther no stryffe,
Till Percyvell had in his lyffe
A son by his yonge wyffe,
   Aftir hym to duelle.
When the childe was borne,
He made calle it one the morne
Als his fadir highte byforne -
   Yonge Percyvell.
The knyghte was fayne a feste made
For knave-childe that he hade;
And sythen, withowtten any bade
   Offe justynges they telle.

Now of justynges they tell:
They sayne that Sir Percyvell
That he will in the felde duelle,
   Als he hase are done.

A grete justynge was ther sett
Of all the kempes that ther mett,
For he wolde his son were gette
   In the same wonne.
Theroff the Rede Knyghte was blythe,
When he herde of that justynge kythe,
And graythed hym armour ful swythe,
   And rode thedir righte sone;
Agayne Percyvell he rade,
With schafte and with schelde brade,
To holde his heste that he made,
   Of maistres to mone.

Now of maistres to mone,
Percyvell hase wele done,
For the love of his yonge sone,
   One the firste day.
Ere the Rede Knyghte was bownn,
Percyvell hase borne downn
Knyght, duke, erle, and baroun,
   And vencusede the play.
Right als he hade done this honour,
So come the Rede Knyghte to the stowre.
Bot "Wo worthe wykkyde armour!"
   Percyvell may say.
For ther was Sir Percyvell slayne,
And the Rede Knyghte fayne -
In herte is noghte for to layne -
   When he went on his way.

When he went on his way,
Durste ther no man to hym say,

Nowther in erneste ne in play,
    To byd hym habyde;
For he had slayne righte thare
The beste body at thare ware,
Sir Percyvell, with woundes sare,
    And stonayed that tyde.
And than thay couthe no better rede
Bot put hym in a prevee stede,
Als that men dose with the dede,
    In erthe for to hyde.
Scho that was his lady
Mighte be full sary,
That lorne hade siche a body:
    Hir aylede no pryde.

And now is Percyvell the wighte
Slayne in batelle and in fyghte,
And the lady hase gyffen a gyfte,
    Holde if scho may,
That scho schall never mare wone
In stede, with hir yonge sone,
Ther dedes of armes schall be done,
    By nyghte ne be daye.
Bot in the wodde schall he be:
Sall he no thyng see
Bot the leves of the tree
    And the greves graye;
Schall he nowther take tent
To justes ne to tournament,
Bot in the wilde wodde went,
    With bestes to playe.

With wilde bestes for to playe,
Scho tuke hir leve and went hir waye,
Bothe at baron and at raye,
  And went to the wodde.
Byhynde scho leved boure and haulle;
A mayden scho tuke hir withalle,
That scho myghte appon calle
  When that hir nede stode.
Other gudes wolde scho nonne nayte,
Bot with hir tuke a tryppe of gayte,
With mylke of tham for to bayte
  To hir lyves fode.
Off all hir lordes faire gere,
Wolde scho noghte with hir bere
Bot a lyttill Scottes spere,
  Agayne hir son yode.

And when hir yong son yode,
Scho bade hym walke in the wodde,
Tuke hym the Scottes spere gude,
  And gaffe hym in hande.
"Swete modir," sayde he,
"What manere of thyng may this bee
That ye nowe hafe taken mee?
  What calle yee this wande?"
Than byspakke the lady:
"Son," scho sayde, "sekerly,
It es a dart doghty;
  In the wodde I it fande."
The childe es payed, of his parte,
His modir hafe gyffen hym that darte;
Therwith made he many marte

In that wodde-lande.

Thus he welke in the lande,
With hys darte in his hande;
Under the wilde wodde-wande
 He wexe and wele thrafe.
He wolde schote with his spere
Bestes and other gere,
As many als he myghte bere.
 He was a gude knave!
Smalle birdes wolde he slo,
Hertys, hyndes also;
Broghte his moder of thoo:
 Thurte hir none crave. I
So wele he lernede hym to schote,
Ther was no beste that welke one fote
To fle fro hym was it no bote.
 When that he wolde hym have,

Even when he wolde hym have.
Thus he wexe and wele thrave,
And was reghte a gude knave
 Within a fewe yere.
Fyftene wynter and mare
He duellede in those holtes hare;
Nowther nurture ne lare
 Scho wolde hym none lere.
Till it byfelle, on a day,
The lady till hir son gun say,
"Swete childe, I rede thou praye
 To Goddes Sone dere,
That he wolde helpe the -

Lorde, for His poustee -
A gude man for to bee,
  And longe to duelle here."

"Swete moder," sayde he,
"Whatkyns a godd may that be
That ye nowe bydd mee
  That I schall to pray?"
Then byspakke the lady even:
"It es the grete Godd of heven:
This worlde made He within seven,
  Appon the sexte day."
"By grete Godd," sayde he than,
"And I may mete with that man,
With alle the crafte that I kan,
  Reghte so schall I pray!"
There he levede in a tayte
Bothe his modir and his gayte,
The grete Godd for to layte,
  Fynde hym when he may.

And as he welke in holtes hare,
He sawe a gate, as it ware;
With thre knyghtis mett he thare
  Off Arthrus in.
One was Ewayne fytz Asoure,
Another was Gawayne with honour,
And Kay, the bolde baratour,
  And all were of his kyn.
In riche robes thay ryde;
The childe hadd no thyng that tyde
That he myghte in his bones hyde,

Bot a gaytes skynn.
He was a burely of body, and therto right brade;
One ayther halfe a skynn he hade;
The hode was of the same made,
    Juste to the chynn.

His hode was juste to his chyn,
The flesche halfe tourned within.
The childes witt was full thyn
    When he scholde say oughte.
Thay were clothede all in grene;
Siche hade he never sene:
Wele he wened that thay had bene
    The Godd that he soghte.
He said, "Wilke of yow alle three
May the grete Godd bee
That my moder tolde mee,
    That all this werlde wroghte?"
Bot than ansuerde Sir Gawayne
Faire and curtaisely agayne,
"Son, so Criste mote me sayne,
    For swilke are we noghte."

Than saide the fole one the filde,
Was comen oute of the woddes wilde,
To Gawayne that was meke and mylde
    And softe to ansuare,
"I sall sla yow all three
Bot ye smertly now telle mee
Whatkyns thynges that ye bee,
    Sen ye no goddes are."
Then ansuerde Sir Kay,

"Who solde we than say
That hade slayne us to-day
  In this holtis hare?"
At Kayes wordes wexe he tene:
Bot he a grete bukke had bene,
Ne hadd he stonde tham bytwene, 2
  He hade hym slayne thare.

Bot than said Gawayn to Kay,
"Thi prowde wordes pares ay;
I scholde wyn this childe with play,
  And thou wolde holde the still.
Swete son," than said he,
"We are knyghtis all thre;
With Kyng Arthoure duelle wee,
  That hovyn es on hyll."
Then said Percyvell the lyghte,
In gayte-skynnes that was dyghte,
"Will Kyng Arthoure make me knyghte,
  And I come hym till?"
Than saide Sir Gawayne righte thare,
"I kane gyffe the nane ansuare;
Bot to the Kynge I rede thou fare,
  To wete his awenn will!"

To wete than the Kynges will
Thare thay hoven yitt still;
The childe hase taken hym till
  For to wende hame.
And als he welke in the wodde,
He sawe a full faire stode
Offe coltes and of meres gude,

Bot never one was tame;
And sone saide he, "Bi Seyne John,
Swilke thynges as are yone
Rade the knyghtes apone;
  Knewe I thaire name,
Als ever mote I thryffe or thee,
The moste of yone that I see
Smertly schall bere mee
  Till I come to my dame."

He saide, "When I come to my dame,
And I fynde hir at hame,
Scho will telle the name
  Off this ilke thynge."
The moste mere he thare see
Smertly overrynnes he,
And saide, "Thou sall bere me
  To-morne to the Kynge."
Kepes he no sadill-gere,
Bot stert up on the mere:
Hamewarde scho gun hym bere,
  Withowtten faylynge.
The lady was never more sore bygone.
Scho wiste never whare to wonne,
When scho wiste hir yonge sonne
  Horse hame brynge.

Scho saw hym horse hame brynge;
Scho wiste wele, by that thynge,
That the kynde wolde oute sprynge
  For thynge that be moughte.
Than als sone saide the lady,

"That ever solde I sorowe dry,
For love of thi body,
  That I hafe dere boghte!
Dere son," saide scho hym to,
"Thou wirkeste thiselfe mekill unroo,
What will thou with this mere do,
  That thou hase hame broghte?"
Bot the boye was never so blythe
Als when he herde the name kythe
Of the stode-mere stythe.
  Of na thyng than he roghte.

Now he calles hir a mere,
Als his moder dide ere;
He wened all other horses were
  And hade bene callede soo.
"Moder, at yonder hill hafe I bene;
Thare hafe I thre knyghtes sene,
And I hafe spoken with tham, I wene,
  Wordes in throo;
I have highte tham all thre
Before thaire Kyng for to be:
Siche on schall he make me
  As is one of tho!"
He sware by grete Goddes myghte,
"I schall holde that I hafe highte;
Bot-if the Kyng make me knyghte,
  To-morne I sall hym sloo!"

Bot than byspakke the lady,
That for hir son was sary -
Hir thoghte wele that scho myght dy

And knelyde one hir knee:
"Sone, thou has takyn thi rede,
To do thiselfe to the dede!
In everilke a strange stede,
   Doo als I bydde the:
To-morne es forthirmaste Yole-day,
And thou says thou will away
To make the knyghte, if thou may,
   Als thou tolde mee.
Lyttill thou can of nurtoure:
Luke thou be of mesure
Bothe in haulle and in boure,
   And fonde to be fre."

Than saide the lady so brighte,
"There thou meteste with a knyghte,
Do thi hode off, I highte,
   And haylse hym·in hy."
"Swete moder," sayd he then,
"I saw never yit no men;
If I solde a knyghte ken,
   Telles me wharby."
Scho schewede hym the menevaire -
Scho had robes in payre.
"Sone, ther thou sees this fare
   In thaire hodes lye."
"Bi grete God," sayd he,
"Where that I a knyghte see,
Moder, as ye bidd me,
   Righte so schall I."

All that nyghte till it was day,

The childe by the modir lay,
Till on the morne he wolde away,
   For thyng that myghte betyde.
Brydill hase he righte nane;
Seese he no better wane,
Bot a wythe hase he tane,
   And kevylles his stede.
His moder gaffe hym a ryng,
And bad he solde agayne it bryng;
"Sonne, this sall be oure takynnyng,
   For here I sall the byde."
He tase the rynge and the spere,
Stirttes up appon the mere:
Fro the moder that hym bere,
   Forthe gan he ryde.

One his way as he gan ryde,
He fande an haulle ther besyde;
He saide, "For oghte that may betyde,
   Thedir in will I."
He went in withowtten lett;
He fande a brade borde sett,
A bryghte fire, wele bett,
   Brynnande therby.
A mawnger ther he fande,
Corne therin lyggande;
Therto his mere he bande
   With the withy.
He saide, "My modir bad me
That I solde of mesure bee
Halfe that I here see
   Styll sall it ly."

The corne he pertis in two,
Gaffe his mere the tone of thoo,
And to the borde gan he goo,
   Certayne that tyde.
He fande a lofe of brede fyne
And a pychere with wyne,
A mese of the kechyne,
   A knyfe ther besyde.
The mete ther that he fande,
He dalte it even with his hande,
Lefte the halfe lyggande
   A felawe to byde.
The tother halfe ete he;
How myghte he more of mesure be?
Faste he fonded to be free,
   Thofe he were of no pryde.

Thofe he were of no pryde,
Forthyrmore gan he glyde
Till a chambir ther besyde,
   Moo sellys to see.
Riche clothes fande he sprede,
A lady slepande on a bedde;
He said, "Forsothe, a tokyn to wedde
   Sall thou lefe with mee."
Ther he kyste that swete thynge;
Of hir fynger he tuke a rynge;
His awenn modir takynnynge
   He lefte with that fre.
He went forthe to his mere,
Tuke with hym his schorte spere,

18

Lepe on lofte, as he was ere;
　His way rydes he.

Now on his way rydes he,
Moo selles to see;
A knyghte wolde he nedis bee,
　Withowtten any bade.
He came ther the Kyng was,
Servede of the firste mese.
To hym was the maste has
　That the childe hade;
And thare made he no lett
At gate, dore, ne wykett,
Bot in graythely he gett -
　Syche maistres he made.
At his firste in-comynge,
His mere, withowtten faylynge,
Kyste the forhevede of the Kynge -
　So nerehande he rade!

The Kyng had ferly thaa,
And up his hande gan he taa
And putt it forthir hym fraa,
　The mouthe of the mere.
He saide, "Faire childe and free,
Stonde still besyde mee,
And tell me wythen that thou bee,
　And what thou will here."
Than said the fole of the filde,
"I ame myn awnn modirs childe,
Comen fro the woddes wylde
　Till Arthure the dere.

19

Yisterday saw I knyghtis three:
Siche on sall thou make mee
On this mere byfor the,
   Thi mete or thou schere!"

Bot than spak Sir Gawayne,
Was the Kynges trenchepayne,
Said, "Forsothe, is noghte to layne,
   I am one of thaa.
Childe, hafe thou my blyssyng
For thi feres folowynge!
Here hase thou fonden the Kynge
   That kan the knyghte maa."
Than sayde Peceyvell the free,
"And this Arthure the Kyng bee,
Luke he a knyghte make mee:
   I rede at it be swaa!"
Thofe he unborely were dyghte,
He sware by mekill Goddes myghte:
"Bot if the Kyng make me knyghte,
   I sall hym here slaa!"

All that ther weren, olde and yynge,
Hadden ferly of the Kyng,
That he wolde suffre siche a thyng
   Of that foull wyghte
On horse hovande hym by.
The Kyng byholdes hym on hy;
Than wexe he sone sory
   When he sawe that syghte.
The teres oute of his eghne glade,
Never one another habade.

"Allas," he sayde, "that I was made,
    Be day or by nyghte,
One lyve I scholde after hym bee
    That me thynke lyke the: 3
Thou arte so semely to see,
    And thou were wele dighte!"

He saide, "And thou were wele dighte,
Thou were lyke to a knyghte
That I lovede with all my myghte
    Whills he was one lyve.
So wele wroghte he my will
In all manere of skill,
I gaffe my syster hym till,
    For to be his wyfe.
He es moste in my mane:
Fiftene yere es it gane,
Sen a theffe hade hym slane
    Abowte a littill stryffe!
Sythen hafe I ever bene his fo,
For to wayte hym with wo.
Bot I myghte hym never slo,
    His craftes are so ryfe."

He sayse, "His craftes are so ryfe,
Ther is no man apon lyfe,
With swerde, spere, ne with knyfe
    May stroye hym allan,
Bot if it were Sir Percyvell son.
Whoso wiste where he ware done!
The bokes says that he mon
    Venge his fader bane."

The childe thoghte he longe bade
That he ne ware a knyghte made,
For he wiste never that he hade
    A fader to be slayne;
The lesse was his menynge.
He saide sone to the Kynge,
"Sir, late be thi jangleynge!
    Of this kepe I nane."

He sais, "I kepe not to stande
With thi jangleyns to lange.
Make me knyghte with thi hande,
    If it sall be done!"
Than the Kyng hym hendly highte
That he schold dub hym to knyghte,
With thi that he wolde doun lighte
    And ete with hym at none.
The Kyng biholdes the vesage free,
And ever more trowed hee
That the childe scholde bee
    Sir Percyvell son:
It ran in the Kynges mode,
His syster Acheflour the gude -
How scho went into the wodde
    With hym for to wonn.

The childe hadde wonnede in the wodde;
He knewe nother evyll ne gude;
The Kynge hymselfe understode
    He was a wilde man.
So faire he spakke hym withall,
He lyghtes doun in the haulle,

Bonde his mere amonge tham alle
　　And to the borde wann.
Bot are he myghte bygynn
To the mete for to wynn,
So commes the Rede Knyghte in
　　Emanges tham righte than,
Prekande one a rede stede;
Blode-rede was his wede.
He made tham gammen full gnede,
　　With craftes that he can.

With his craftes gan he calle,
And callede tham recrayhandes all,
Kynge, knyghtes inwith walle,
　　At the bordes ther thay bade.
Full felly the coupe he fett,
Bifore the Kynge that was sett.
Ther was no man that durste hym lett,
　　Thofe that he were fadde.
The couppe was filled full of wyne;
He dranke of that that was therinn.
All of rede golde fyne
　　Was the couppe made.
He tuke it up in his hande,
The coupe that he there fande,
And lefte tham all sittande,
　　And fro tham he rade.

Now from tham he rade,
Als he says that this made.
The sorowe that the Kynge hade

Mighte no tonge tell.
"A! dere God," said the Kyng than,
"That all this wyde werlde wan,
Whethir I sall ever hafe that man
    May make yone fende duelle?
Fyve yeres hase he thus gane,
And my coupes fro me tane,
And my gude knyghte slayne,
    Men calde Sir Percyvell;
Sythen taken hase he three,
And ay awaye will he bee,
Or I may harnayse me
    In felde hym to felle."

"Petir!" quod Percyvell the yonge,
"Hym than will I down dynge
And the coupe agayne brynge,
    And thou will make me knyghte."
"Als I am trewe kyng," said he,
"A knyghte sall I make the,
Forthi thou will brynge mee
    The coupe of golde bryghte."
Up ryses Sir Arthoure,
Went to a chamboure
To feche doun armoure,
    The childe in to dyghte;
Bot are it was doun caste,
Ere was Percyvell paste,
And on his way folowed faste,
    That he solde with fyghte.

With his foo for to fighte,

None othergates was he dighte,
Bot in thre gayt-skynnes righte,
   A fole als he ware.

He cryed, "How, man on thi mere!
Bryng agayne the Kynges gere,
Or with my dart I sall the fere
   And make the unfere!"
And after the Rede Knyghte he rade,
Baldely, withowtten bade:
Sayd, "A knyght I sall be made
   For som of thi gere."
He sware by mekill Goddes payne,
"Bot if thou brynge the coupe agayne,
With my dart thou sall be slayne
   And slongen of thi mere."
The kynghte byhaldes hym in throo,
Calde hym fole that was hys foo,
For he named hym soo -
   The stede that hym bere.

And for to see hym with syghte,
He putt his umbrere on highte,
To byhalde how he was dyghte,
   That so till hym spake.
He sayde, "Come I to the, appert fole;
I sall caste the in the pole,
For all the heghe days of Yole,
   Als ane olde sakke."
Than sayd Percyvell the free,
"Be I fole, or whatte I bee,

Now sone of that sall wee see
   Whose browes schall blakke."
Of schottyng was the childe slee:
At the knyghte lete he flee,
Smote hym in at the eghe
   And oute at the nakke.

For the dynt that he tuke,
Oute of sadill he schoke,
Whoso the sothe will luke,
   And ther was he slayne.
He falles down one the hill;
His stede rynnes whare he will.
Than saide Percyvell hym till,
   "Thou art a lethir swayne."
Then saide the childe in that tyde,
"And thou woldeste me here byde,
After thi mere scholde I ryde
   And brynge hir agayne;
Then myghte we bothe with myghte
Menskfully togedir fyghte,
Ayther of us, as he were a knyghte,
   Till tyme the tone ware slayne."

Now es the Rede Knyghte slayne,
Lefte dede in the playne.
The childe gon his mere mayne
   After the stede.
The stede was swifter than the mere,
For he hade no thynge to bere
Bot his sadill and his gere,
   Fro hym thofe he yede.

The mere was bagged with fole;
And hirselfe a grete bole;
For to rynne scho myghte not thole,
   Ne folowe hym no spede.
The childe saw that it was soo,
And till his fete he gan hym too;
The gates that he scholde goo
   Made he full gnede.

The gates made he full gnede
In the waye ther he yede;
With strenght tuke he the stede
   And broghte to the knyghte.
"Me thynke," he sayde, "thou arte fele
That thou ne will away stele;
Now I houppe that thou will dele
   Strokes appon hyghte.
I hafe broghte to the thi mere
And mekill of thyn other gere;
Lepe on hir, as thou was ere,
   And thou will more fighte!"
The knyghte lay still in the stede:
What sulde he say, when he was dede?
The childe couthe no better rede,
   Bot down gun he lyghte.

Now es Percyvell lyghte
To unspoyle the Rede Knyghte,
Bot he ne couthe never fynd righte
   The lacynge of his wede.
He was armede so wele
In gude iryn and in stele,

27

He couthe no gett of a dele,
   For nonkyns nede.
He sayd, "My moder bad me,
When my dart solde broken be,
Owte of the iren bren the tree:
   Now es me fyre gnede."
Now he getis hym flynt,
His fyre-iren he hent,
And then, withowtten any stynt,
   He kyndilt a glede.

Now he kyndils a glede,
Amonge the buskes he yede
And gedirs, full gude spede,
   Wodde, a fyre to make.
A grete fyre made he than,
The Rede Knyghte in to bren,
For he ne couthe nott ken
   His gere off to take.
Be than was Sir Gawayne dyght,
Folowede after the fyghte
Betwene hym and the Rede Knyghte,
   For the childes sake.
He fande the Rede Knyght lyggand,
Slayne of Percyvell hande,
Besyde a fyre brynnande
   Off byrke and of akke.

Ther brent of birke and of ake
Gret brandes and blake.
"What wylt thou with this fyre make?"

28

Sayd Gawayne hym till.
"Petir!" quod Percyvell then,
"And I myghte hym thus ken,
Out of his iren I wolde hym bren
   Righte here on this hill."
Bot then sayd Sir Gawayne,
"The Rede Knyghte for thou has slayne,
I sall unarme hym agayne,
   And thou will holde the still."
Than Sir Gawayn doun lyghte,
Unlacede the Rede Knyghte;
The childe in his armour dight
   At his awnn will.

When he was dighte in his atire,
He tase the knyghte bi the swire,
Keste hym reghte in the fyre,
   The brandes to balde.
Bot then said Percyvell on bost,
"Ly still therin now and roste!
I kepe nothynge of thi coste,
   Ne noghte of thi spalde!"
The knyghte lygges ther on brede;
The childe es dighte in his wede,
And lepe up apon his stede,
   Als hymselfe wolde.
He luked doun to his fete,
Saw his gere faire and mete:
"For a knyghte I may be lete
   And myghte be calde."

Then sayd Sir Gawayn hym till,

"Goo we faste fro this hill!
Thou hase done what thou will;
    It neghes nere nyghte."
"What! trowes thou," quod Percyvell the yonge,
"That I will agayn brynge
Untill Arthoure the Kynge
    The golde that es bryghte?
Nay, so mote I thryfe or thee,
I am als grete a lorde als he;
To-day ne schall he make me
    None other gates knyghte.
Take the coupe in thy hande
And mak thiselfe the presande,
For I will forthire into the lande,
    Are I doun lyghte."

Nowther wolde he doun lyghte,
Ne he wolde wende with the knyght,
Bot rydes forthe all the nyghte,
    So prowde was he than.
Till on the morne at forthe dayes,
He mett a wyche, as men says.
His horse and his harnays
    Couthe scho wele ken.
Scho wende that it hade bene
The Rede Knyghte that scho hade sene,
Was wonnt in those armes to bene,
    To gerre the stede rynne.
In haste scho come hym agayne,
Sayde, "It is not to layne,
Men tolde me that thou was slayne
    With Arthours men.

Ther come one of my men,
Till yonder hill he gan me kenne,
There thou sees the fyre brene,
   And sayde that thou was thare."
Ever satt Percyvell stone-still,
And spakke no thynge hir till
Till scho hade sayde all hir will,
   And spakke lesse ne mare.
"At yondere hill hafe I bene:
Nothynge hafe I there sene
Bot gayte-skynnes, I wene.
   Siche ill-farande fare!"
"Mi sone, and thou ware thare slayne
And thyn armes of drawen,
I couthe hele the agayne
   Als wele als thou was are."

Than wist Percyvell by thatt,
It servede hym of somwhatt,
The wylde fyre that he gatt
   When the knyghte was slayne;
And righte so wolde he, thare
That the olde wiche ware.
Oppon his spere he hir bare
   To the fyre agayne;
In ill wrethe and in grete,
He keste the wiche in the hete;
He sayde, "Ly still and swete
   Bi thi son, that lyther swayne!"
Thus he leves thaym twoo,
And on his gates gan he goo:

Siche dedis to do moo
 Was the childe fayne.

Als he come by a wodd-syde,
He sawe ten men ryde;
He said, "For oughte that may betyde,
 To tham will I me."
When those ten saw hym thare,
Thay wende the Rede Knyghte it ware,
That wolde tham all forfare,
 And faste gan thay flee;
For he was sogates cledde,
Alle belyffe fro hym thay fledde;
And ever the faster that thay spedde,
 The swiftlyere sewed hee,
Till he was warre of a knyghte,
And of the menevaire he had syght;
He put up his umbrere on hight,
 And said, "Sir, God luke thee!"

The childe sayde, "God luke the!"
The knyght said, "Now wele the be!
A, lorde Godd, now wele es mee
 That ever was I made!"
For by the vesage hym thoghte
The Rede Knyghte was it noghte,
That hade them all bysoughte;
 And baldely he bade.
It semede wele bi the syghte
That he had slayne the Rede Knyght:
In his armes was he dighte,

And on his stede rade.
"Son," sayde the knyghte tho,
And thankede the childe full thro,
"Thou hase slayne the moste foo
   That ever yitt I hade."

Then sayde Percyvell the free,
"Wherefore fledde yee
Lange are, when ye sawe mee
   Come rydande yow by?"
Bot than spake the olde knyghte,
That was paste out of myghte
With any man for to fyghte:
   He ansuerde in hy;
He sayde, "Theis children nyne,
All are thay sonnes myne.
For ferde or I solde tham tyne,
   Therfore fledd I.
We wende wele that it had bene
The Rede Knyghte that we hade sene;
He walde hafe slayne us bydene,
   Withowtten mercy.

Withowtten any mercy
He wolde hafe slayne us in hy;
To my sonnes he hade envy
   Moste of any men.
Fiftene yeres es it gane
Syn he my brodire hade slane;
Now hadde the theefe undirtane
   To sla us all then:
He was ferde lesse my sonnes sold hym slo

When thay ware eldare and moo,
And that thay solde take hym for thaire foo
  Where thay myghte hym ken;
Hade I bene in the stede
Ther he was done to the dede,
I solde never hafe etyn brede
  Are I hade sene hym bren."

"Petir!" quod Percyvell, "he es brende!
I haffe spedde better than I wend
Ever at the laste ende."
  The blythere wexe the knyghte;
By his haulle thaire gates felle,
And yerne he prayed Percyvell
That he solde ther with hym duelle
  And be ther all that nyghte.
Full wele he couthe a geste calle.
He broghte the childe into the haulle;
So faire he spake hym withalle
  That he es doun lyghte;
His stede es in stable sett
And hymselfe to the haulle fett,
And than, withowtten any lett,
  To the mette thay tham dighte.

Mete and drynke was ther dighte,
And men to serve tham full ryghte;
The childe that come with the knyghte,
  Enoghe ther he fande.
At the mete as thay beste satte,
Come the portere fro the gate,
Saide a man was theratte

Of the Maydenlande;
Saide, "Sir, he prayes the
Off mete and drynke, for charyté;
For a messagere es he
    And may nott lange stande."
The knyght badde late hym inn,
"For," he sayde, "it es no synn,
The man that may the mete wynn
To gyffe the travellande."

Now the travellande man
The portere lete in than;
He haylsede the knyghte as he can,
    Als he satt on dese.
The knyghte askede hym thare
Whase man that he ware,
And how ferre that he walde so fare,
    Withowtten any lese.
He saide, "I come fro the Lady Lufamour,
That sendes me to Kyng Arthoure,
And prayes hym, for his honoure,
    Hir sorowes for to sesse.
Up resyn es a Sowdane:
Alle hir landes hase he tane;
So byseges he that woman
    That scho may hafe no pese."

He sayse that scho may have no pese,
The lady, for hir fayrenes,
And for hir mekill reches.
    "He wirkes hir full woo;
He dose hir sorow all hir sythe,

35

And all he slaes doun rythe;
He wolde have hir to wyfe,
   And scho will noghte soo.
Now hase that ilke Sowdane
Hir fadir and hir eme slane,
And hir brethir ilkane,
   And is hir moste foo.
So nere he hase hir now soughte
That till a castelle es scho broghte,
And fro the walles will he noghte,
   Ere that he may hir too.

The Sowdane sayse he will hir ta;
The lady will hirselfe sla
Are he, that es hir maste fa,
   Solde wedde hir to wyfe.
Now es the Sowdan so wyghte,
Alle he slaes doun ryghte:
Ther may no man with hym fyghte,
   Bot he were kempe ryfe."
Than sayde Percyvell, "I the praye,
That thou wolde teche me the waye
Thedir, als the gates laye,
   Withowtten any stryfe;
Mighte I mete with that Sowdan
That so dose to that woman,
Alsone he solde be slane,
   And I myghte hafe the lyfe!"

The messangere prayed hym mare
That he wolde duell still thare:

"For I will to the Kynge fare,
    Myne erandes for to say.
For then mekill sorowe me betyde,
And I lenger here habyde,
Bot ryghte now will I ryde,
    Als so faste als I may."
The knyghte herde hym say so;
Yerne he prayes hym to too
His nyne sonnes, with hym to goo.
    He nykkes hym with nay.
Bot so faire spekes he
That he takes of tham three,
In his felawchipe to be -
    The blythere were thay.

Thay ware blythe of ther bade,
Busked tham and forthe rade;
Mekill myrthes thay made:
    Bot lyttill it amende.
He was paste bot a while -
The montenance of a myle -
He was bythoghte of a gyle
    Wele werse than thay wende.
Thofe thay ware of thaire fare fayne,
Forthwarde was thaire cheftayne;
Ever he sende on agayne
    At ilke a myle ende,
Untill thay ware alle gane;
Than he rydes hym allane
Als he ware sprongen of a stane,
    Thare na man hym kende,

For he walde none sold hym ken.
Forthe rydes he then,
Amanges uncouthe men
   His maystres to make.
Now hase Percyvell in throo
Spoken with his emes twoo,
Bot never one of thoo
   Took his knawlage.
Now in his way es he sett
That may hym lede, withowtten lett,
Thare he and the Sowdan sall mete,
   His browes to blake.
Late we Percyvell the yynge
Fare in Goddes blyssynge,
And untill Arthoure the Kynge
   Will we agayne take.

The gates agayne we will tane:
The Kyng to care-bedd es gane;
For mournynge es his maste mane.
   He syghes full sore.
His wo es wansome to wreke,
His hert es bownn for to breke,
For he wend never to speke
   With Percyvell no more.
Als he was layde for to ly,
Come the messangere on hy
With lettres fro the lady,
   And schewes tham righte thare.
Afote myghte the Kyng noght stande,
Bot rede tham thare lyggande,
And sayde, "Of thyne erande

Thou hase thyn answare."

He sayde, "Thou wote thyne ansuare:
The mane that es seke and sare,
He may full ill ferre fare
  In felde for to fyghte."
The messangere made his mone:
Saide, "Wo worthe wikkede wone!
Why ne hade I tournede and gone
  Agayne with the knyghte?"
"What knyghte es that," said the Kyng,
"That thou mase of thy menynge?
In my londe wot I no lordyng
  Es worthy to be a knyghte."
The messangere ansuerd agayne,
"Wete ye, his name es for to layne,
The whethir I wolde hafe weten fayne
  What the childe highte.

Thus mekill gatt I of that knyght:
His dame sonne, he said, he hight.
One what maner that he was dight
  Now I sall yow telle:
He was wighte and worthly,
His body bolde and borely,
His armour bryghte and blody -
  Hade bene late in batell;
Blode-rede was his stede,
His akton, and his other wede;
His cote of the same hede
  That till a knyghte felle."
Than comanded the Kyng

Horse and armes for to brynge:
"If I kan trow thi talkynge,
   That ilke was Percyvell."

For the luffe of Percyvell,
To horse and armes thay felle;
Thay wolde no lengare ther duelle:
   To fare ware thay fayne.
Faste forthe gan thay fare;
Thay were aferde full sare,
Ere thay come whare he ware,
   The childe wolde be slayne.
The Kyng tase with hym knyghtis thre:
The ferthe wolde hymselfe be;
Now so faste rydes hee,
   May folowe hym no swayne.
The Kyng es now in his waye;
Lete hym come when he maye!
And I will forthir in my playe
   To Percyvell agayne.

Go we to Percyvell agayne.
The childe paste oute on the playne,
Over more and mountayne,
   To the Maydenlande;
Till agayne the even-tyde,
Bolde bodys sawe he byde,
Pavelouns mekill and unryde
   Aboute a cyté stonde.
On huntyng was the Sowdane;
He lefte men many ane,

Twenty score that wele kan:
  Be the gates yemande -
Elleven score one the nyghte,
And ten one the daye-lighte -
Wele armyde at alle righte,
  With wapyns in hande.

With thaire wapyns in thaire hande,
There will thay fight ther thay stande,
Sittande and lyggande,
  Elleven score of men.
In he rydes one a rase,
Or that he wiste where he was,
Into the thikkeste of the prese
  Amanges tham thanne.
And up stirt one that was bolde,
Bygane his brydill to holde,
And askede whedire that he wolde
  Make his horse to rynne.
He said, "I ame hedir come
For to see a Sowdane;
In faythe, righte sone he sall be slane,
  And I myghte hym ken.

If I hym oghte ken may,
To-morne, when it es lighte daye
Than sall we togedir playe
  With wapyns unryde."
They herde that he had undirtane
For to sle thaire Sowdane.
Thay felle aboute hym, everilkane,
  To make that bolde habyde.

The childe sawe that he was fade,
The body that his bridill hade:
Even over hym he rade,
   In gate there bisyde.
He stayred about hym with his spere;
Many thurgh gane he bere:
Ther was none that myght hym dere,
   Percevell, that tyde.

Tide in townne who will telle,
Folkes undir his fete felle;
The bolde body Percevelle,
   He sped tham to spill.
Hym thoghte no spede at his spere:
Many thurgh gane he bere,
Fonde folke in the here,
   Feghtyng to fill.
Fro that it was mydnyghte
Till it was even at daye-lighte,
Were thay never so wilde ne wighte,
   He wroghte at his will.
Thus he dalt with his brande,
There was none that myght hym stande
Halfe a dynt of his hande
   That he stroke till.

Now he strykes for the nonys,
Made the Sarazenes hede-bones
Hoppe als dose hayle-stones
   Abowtte one the gres;
Thus he dalt tham on rawe
Till the daye gun dawe:

He layd thaire lyves full law,
   Als many als there was.
When he hade slayne so many men,
He was so wery by then,
I tell yow for certen,
   He roghte wele the lesse
Awther of lyfe or of dede;
To medis that he were in a stede
Thar he myghte riste hym in thede
   A stownde in sekirnes.

Now fonde he no sekirnes,
Bot under the walle ther he was,
A faire place he hym chese,
   And down there he lighte.
He laide hym doun in that tyde;
His stede stode hym besyde:
The fole was fayne for to byde -
   Was wery for the fyght
Till one the morne that it was day.
The wayte appon the walle lay:
He sawe an uggly play
   In the place dighte;
Yitt was ther more ferly:
Ther was no qwyk man left therby!
Thay called up the lady
   For to see that sighte.

Now commes the lady to that sight,
The Lady Lufamour, the brighte;
Scho clambe up to the walle on hight

Full faste to beholde;
Hedes and helmys ther was
(I tell yow withowtten lese),
Many layde one the gresse,
  And many schelde brode.
Grete ferly thaym thoghte
Who that wondir had wroghte,
That had tham to dede broghte,
  That folke in the felde,
And wold come none innermare
For to kythe what he ware,
And wist the lady was thare,
  Thaire warysoune to yelde.

Scho wold thaire warysone yelde:
Full faste forthe thay bihelde
If thay myghte fynde in the felde
  Who hade done that dede;
Thay luked undir thair hande,
Sawe a mekill horse stande,
A blody knyghte liggande
  By a rede stede.
Then said the lady so brighte,
"Yondir ligges a knyghte
That hase bene in the fighte,
  If I kane righte rede;
Owthir es yone man slane,
Or he slepis hym allane,
Or he in batelle es tane,
  For blody are his wede."

Scho says, "Blody are his wede,

44

And so es his riche stede;
Siche a knyght in this thede
  Saw I never nane.
What so he es, and he maye ryse,
He es large there he lyse,
And wele made in alle wyse,
  Ther als man sall be tane."
Scho calde appon hir chaymbirlayne,
Was called hende Hatlayne -
The curtasye of Wawayne
  He weldis in wane;
Scho badd hym, "Wende and see
Yif yon man on lyfe be.
Bid hym com and speke with me,
  And pray hym als thou kane."

Now to pray hym als he kane,
Undir the wallis he wane;
Warly wakend he that mane:
  The horse stode still.
Als it was tolde unto me,
He knelid down on his kne;
Hendely hailsed he that fre,
  And sone said hym till,
"My lady, lele Lufamour,
Habyddis the in hir chambour,
Prayes the, for thyn honour,
  To come, yif ye will."
So kyndly takes he that kyth
That up he rose and went hym wyth,
The man that was of myche pyth
  Hir prayer to fulfill.

Now hir prayer to fulfill,
He folowed the gentilmans will,
And so he went hir untill,
   Forthe to that lady.
Full blythe was that birde brighte
When scho sawe hym with syghte,
For scho trowed that he was wighte,
   And askede hym in hy:
At that fre gan scho frayne,
Thoghe he were lefe for to layne,
If he wiste who had tham slayne -
   Thase folkes of envy.
He sayd, "I soghte none of tho;
I come the Sowdane to slo,
And thay ne wolde noghte late me go;
Thaire lyfes there refte I."

He sayd, "Belyfe thay solde aby."
And Lufamour, that lele lady,
Wist ful wele therby
   The childe was full wighte.
The birde was blythe of that bade
That scho siche and helpe hade;
Agayne the Sowdane was fade
   With alle for to fighte.
Faste the lady hym byhelde:
Scho thoght hym worthi to welde,
And he myghte wyn hir in felde,
   With maystry and myghte.
His stede thay in stabill set
And hymselfe to haulle was fet,

And than, withowtten any let,
   To dyne gun thay dighte.

The childe was sett on the dese,
And served with reches -
I tell yow withowtten lese -
   That gaynely was get,
In a chayere of golde
Bifore the fayrest, to byholde
The myldeste mayden one molde,
   At mete als scho satt.
Scho made hym semblande so gude,
Als thay felle to thaire fude,
The mayden mengede his mode
   With myrthes at the mete,
That for hir sake righte tha
Sone he gane undirta
The sory Sowdane to sla,
   Withowtten any lett.

He sayd, withowtten any lett,
"When the Sowdane and I bene mett,
A sadde stroke I sall one hym sett,
   His pride for to spyll."
Then said the lady so free,
"Who that may his bon be
Sall hafe this kyngdome and me,
   To welde at his will."
He ne hade dyned bot smalle
When worde come into the haulle
That many men withalle

Were hernyste one the hill;
For tene thaire felawes were slayne,
The cité hafe thay nere tane.
The men that were within the wane
  The comon-belle gun knylle.

Now knyllyn thay the comon-belle.
Worde come to Percevell,
And he wold there no lengere duelle,
  Bot lepe fro the dese -
Siche wilde gerys hade he mo -
Sayd, "Kynsmen, now I go.
For alle yone sall I slo
  Longe are I sese!"
Scho kiste hym withowtten lett;
The helme on his hede scho sett;
To the stabill full sone he gett,
  There his stede was.
There were none with hym to fare;
For no man then wolde he spare! -
Rydis furthe, withowtten mare,
  Till he come to the prese.

When he come to the prese,
He rydes in one a rese;
The folkes, that byfore hym was,
  Thaire strenght hade thay tone;
To kepe hym than were thay ware;
Thaire dynttis deris hym no mare
Then whoso hade strekyn sare
  One a harde stone.
Were thay wighte, were thay woke,

Alle that he till stroke,
He made thaire bodies to roke:
   Was ther no better wone.
I wote, he sped hym so sone
That day, by heghe none
With all that folke hade he done:
   One lefe lefte noghte one.

When he had slayne all tho,
He loked forthir hym fro,
If he myghte fynde any mo
   With hym for to fyghte;
And als that hardy bihelde,
He sese, ferre in the felde,
Fowre knyghtis undir schelde
   Come rydand full righte.
One was Kyng Arthour,
Anothir Ewayne, the floure,
The thirde Wawayne with honoure,
   And Kay, the kene knyghte.
Percevell saide, withowtten mare,
"To yondir foure will I fare;
And if the Sowdane be thare,
   I sall holde that I highte."

Now to holde that he hase highte,
Agaynes thaym he rydis righte,
And ay lay the lady brighte
   One the walle, and byhelde
How many men that he had slane,
And sythen gane his stede mayne
Foure kempys agayne,

Forthir in the felde.
Then was the lady full wo
When scho sawe hym go
Agaynes foure knyghtys tho,
   With schafte and with schelde.
They were so mekyl and unryde
That wele wende scho that tyde
With bale thay solde gare hym byde
   That was hir beste belde.

Thofe he were beste of hir belde,
As that lady byhelde,
He rydes forthe in the felde,
   Even tham agayne.
Then sayd Arthoure the Kyng,
"I se a bolde knyghte owt spryng;
For to seke feghtyng,
   Forthe will he frayne.
If he fare forthe to fighte
And we foure kempys agayne one knyght,
Littill menske wold to us lighte
   If he were sone slayne."
They fore forthward right faste,
And sone kevells did thay caste,
And evyr fell it to frayste
Untill Sir Wawayne.

When it felle to Sir Wawayne
To ryde Percevell agayne,
Of that fare was he fayne,
   And fro tham he rade.
Ever the nerre hym he drewe,

Wele the better he hym knewe,
Horse and hernays of hewe,
That the childe hade.
"A, dere God!" said Wawayne the fre,
"How-gates may this be?
If I sle hym, or he me,
    That never yit was fade,
And we are sisters sones two,
And aythir of us othir slo,
He that lifes will be full wo
    That ever was he made."

Now no maistrys he made,
Sir Wawayne, there als he rade,
Bot hovyde styll and habade
    His concell to ta.
"Ane unwyse man," he sayd, "am I,
That puttis myselfe to siche a foly;
Es there no man so hardy
    That ne anothir es alswa.
Thogfe Percevell hase slayne the Rede Knight,
Yitt may another be als wyghte,
And in that gere be dyghte,
    And taken alle hym fra.
If I suffire my sister sone,
And anothir in his gere be done
And gete the maystry me appon,
    That wolde do me wa;

It wolde wirke me full wa!
So mote I one erthe ga,

It ne sall noghte betyde me swa,
   If I may righte rede!
A schafte sall I one hym sett,
And I sall fonde firste to hitt;
Then sall I ken be my witt
   Who weldys that wede."
No more carpys he that tyde,
Bot son togedyr gon thay ryde-
Men that bolde were to byde,
   And styff appon stede;
Thaire horse were stallworthe and strange,
Thair scheldis were unfailande;
Thaire speris brake to thaire hande,
   Als tham byhoved nede.

Now es broken that are were hale,
And than bygane Percevale
For to tell one a tale
   That one his tonge laye.
He sayde, "Wyde-whare hafe I gane;
Siche anothir Sowdane
In faythe sawe I never nane,
   By nyghte ne by daye.
I hafe slayne, and I the ken,
Twenty score of thi men;
And of alle that I slewe then,
   Me thoghte it bot a playe
Agayne that dynt that I hafe tane;
For siche one aughte I never nane
Bot I qwyte two for ane,
   Forsothe, and I maye."

Then spake Sir Wawayne -
Certanely, is noghte to layne -
Of that fare was he fayne,
   In felde there thay fighte:
By the wordis so wylde
At the fole one the felde,
He wiste wele it was the childe,
   Percevell the wighte -
He sayse, "I ame no Sowdane,
Bot I am that ilke man
That thi body bygan
   In armours to dighte.
I giffe the prise to thi pyth.
Unkyndely talked thou me with:
My name es Wawayne in kythe,
   Whoso redys righte."

He sayes, "Who that will rede the aryghte,
My name es Wawayne the knyghte."
And than thay sessen of thaire fighte,
   Als gude frendes scholde.
He sayse, "Thynkes thou noghte when
That thou woldes the knyghte brene,
For thou ne couthe noghte ken
   To spoyle hym alle colde?"
Bot then was Percevell the free
Als blythe als he myghte be,
For then wiste he wele that it was he,
   By takens that he tolde.
He dide then als he gane hym lere:
Putt up hys umbrere;
And kyste togedir with gud chere

Those beryns so bolde.

Now kissede the beryns so bolde,
Sythen talkede what thay wolde.
Be then come Arthour the bolde,
   That there was knyghte and kyng
Als his cosyns hadd done,
Thankede God also sone.
Off mekill myrthis thay mone
   At thaire metyng.
Sythen, withowtten any bade,
To the castelle thay rade
With the childe that thay hade,
   Percevell the yynge.
The portere was redy thare,
Lete the knyghtis in fare;
A blythere lady than . . .
   . . . .

"Mi grete socour at thou here sende,
Off my castell me to diffende,
Agayne the Sowdane to wende,
   That es my moste foo."
Theire stedis thay sett in the stalle.
The Kyng wendis to haulle;
His knyghtis yode hym with alle,
   Als kynde was to go.
Thaire metis was redy,
And therto went thay in hy,
The Kyng and the lady,
   And knyghtis also.

Wele welcomed scho the geste
With riche metis of the beste,
Drynkes of the derreste,
  Dighted bydene.
Thay ete and dranke what thay wolde,
Sythen talked and tolde
Off othir estres full olde,
  The Kyng and the Qwene.
At the firste bygynnyng,
Scho frayned Arthour the Kyng
Of childe Percevell the yyng,
  What life he had in bene.
Grete wondir had Lufamour
He was so styffe in stour
And couthe so littill of nurtour
  Als scho had there sene.

Scho had sene with the childe
No thyng bot werkes wylde:
Thoghte grete ferly on filde
  Of that foly fare.
Then said Arthour the Kyng
Of bold Percevell techyng,
Fro the firste bygynnyng
  Till that he come thar:
How his fadir was slayne,
And his modir to the wode gane
For to be there hir allane
  In the holtis hare,
Fully feftene yere
To play hym with the wilde dere:
Littill wonder it were

Wilde if he ware!

When he had tolde this tale
To that semely in sale
He hade wordis at wale
  To tham ilkane.
Then said Percevell the wighte,
"Yif I be noghte yitt knyghte,
Thou sall halde that thou highte,
  For to make me ane."
Than saide the Kyng full sone,
"Ther sall other dedis be done,
And thou sall wynn thi schone
  Appon the Sowdane."
Then said Percevell the fre,
"Als sone als I the Sowdane see,
Righte so sall it sone be,
  Als I hafe undirtane."

He says, "Als I hafe undirtane
For to sla the Sowdane,
So sall I wirke als I kanne,
  That dede to bygynn."
That day was ther no more dede
With those worthily in wede,
Bot buskede tham and to bedde yede,
  The more and the mynn;
Till one the morne erely
Comes the Sowdane with a cry,
Fonde all his folkes hym by
  Putt into pyn.
Sone asked he wha

That so durste his men sla,
And wete hym one lyfe gaa,
   The maystry to wynn.

Now to wynn the maystry,
To the castell gan he cry,
If any were so hardy,
   The maistry to wynn:
"A man for ane,
Thoghe he hadd all his folke slane,
Here sall he fynde Golrotherame
   To mete hym full ryghte,
Appon siche a covenande
That ye hefe up your hande;
Who that may the better stande
   And more es of myghte
To bryng that other to the dede,
Browke wele the londe on brede
And hir that is so faire and rede,
   Lufamour the brighte!"

Then the Kyng Arthour
And the Lady Lufamour
And all that were in the towre
   Graunted therwith.
Thay called Percevell the wight;
The Kyng doubbed hym to knyghte.
Thofe he couthe littill insighte,
   The childe was of pith.
He bad he solde be to prayse,
Therto hende and curtayse;
Sir Percevell the Galayse

Thay called hym in kythe.
Kyng Arthour in Maydenlande
Dubbid hym knyghte with his hande,
Bad hym ther he his fo fande
    To gyff hym no grythe.

Grith takes he nane:
He rydes agayne the Sowdane
That highte Gollerotherame,
    That felle was in fighte.
In the felde so brade,
No more carpynge thay made,
Bot sone togedir thay rade,
    Theire schaftes to righte.
Gollerotheram, thofe he wolde wede,
Percevell bere hym fro his stede
Two londis one brede,
    With maystry and myghte.
At the erthe the Sowdane lay;
His stede gun rynn away;
Than said Percevell one play,
    "Thou haste that I the highte."

He sayd, "I highte the a dynt,
And now, me thynke, thou hase it hynt.
And I may, als I hafe mynt,
    Thou schalt it never mende."
Appon the Sowdan he duelled
To the grownde ther he was felled,
And to the erthe he hym helde
    With his speres ende.
Fayne wolde he hafe hym slayne,

This uncely Sowdane,
Bot gate couthe he get nane,
  So ill was he kende.
Than thynkes the childe
Of olde werkes full wylde:
"Hade I a fire now in this filde,
  Righte here he solde be brende."

He said, "Righte here I solde the brene,
And thou ne solde never more then
Fighte for no wymman,
  So I solde the fere!"
Then said Wawayne the knyghte,
"Thou myghte, and thou knewe righte,
And thou woldes of thi stede lighte,
  Wynn hym one were."
The childe was of gamen gnede;
Now he thynkes one thede,
"Lorde! whethir this be a stede
  I wende had bene a mere?"
In stede righte there he in stode,
He ne wiste nother of evyll ne gude,
Bot then chaunged his mode
  And slaked his spere.

When his spere was up tane,
Then gan this Gollerothiram,
This ilke uncely Sowdane,
  One his fete to gete.
Than his swerde drawes he,
Strykes at Percevell the fre.
The childe hadd no powsté

His laykes to lett.
The stede was his awnn will:
Saw the swerde come hym till,
Leppe up over an hill,
   Fyve stryde mett.
Als he sprent forby,
The Sowdan keste up a cry;
The childe wann owt of study
   That he was inn sett.

Now ther he was in sett,
Owt of study he gett,
And lightis downn, withowtten lett,
   Agaynes hym to goo.
He says, "Now hase thou taughte me
How that I sall wirke with the."
Than his swerde drawes he
   And strake to hym thro.
He hitt hym even one the nekk-bane,
Thurgh ventale and pesane.
The hede of the Sowdane
   He strykes the body fra.
Then full wightly he yode
To his stede, there he stode;
The milde mayden in mode,
   Mirthe may scho ma!

Many mirthes then he made;
In to the castell he rade,
And boldly he there habade
   With that mayden brighte.
Fayne were thay ilkane

That he had slane the Sowdane
And wele wonn that wymman,
   With maystry and myghte.
Thay said Percevell the yyng
Was beste worthy to be kyng,
For wele withowtten lesyng
   He helde that he highte.
Ther was no more for to say,
Bot sythen, appon that other day,
He weddys Lufamour the may,
   This Percevell the wighte.

Now hase Percevell the wight
Wedded Lufamour the bright,
And is a kyng full righte
   Of alle that lande brade.
Than Kyng Arthour in hy
Wolde no lengare ther ly:
Toke lefe at the lady.
   Fro tham than he rade:
Left Percevell the yyng
Off all that lande to be kyng,
For he had with a ryng
   The mayden that it hade. 4
Sythen, appon the tother day,
The Kyng went on his way,
The certane sothe, als I say,
   Withowtten any bade.

Now than yong Percevell habade
In those borowes so brade

For hir sake, that he hade
    Wedd with a ryng.
Wele weldede he that lande,
Alle bowes to his honde;
The folke, that he byfore fonde,
    Knewe hym for kyng.
Thus he wonnes in that wone
Till that the twelmonthe was gone,
With Lufamour his lemman.
    He thoghte on no thyng,
Now on his moder that was,
How scho levyde with the gres,
With more drynke and lesse,
    In welles, there thay spryng.

Drynkes of welles, ther thay spryng,
And gresse etys, withowt lesyng!
Scho liffede with none othir thyng
    In the holtes hare.
Till it byfelle appon a day,
Als he in his bedd lay,
Till hymselfe gun he say,
    Syghande full sare,
"The laste Yole-day that was,
Wilde wayes I chese:
My modir all manles
    Leved I thare."
Than righte sone saide he,
"Blythe sall I never be
Or I may my modir see,
    And wete how scho fare."

Now to wete how scho fare,
The knyght busked hym yare;
He wolde no lengare duelle thare
  For noghte that myghte bee.
Up he rose in that haulle,
Tuke his lefe at tham alle,
Both at grete and at smalle;
  Fro thaym wendis he.
Faire scho prayed hym even than,
Lufamour, his lemman,
Till the heghe dayes of Yole were gane,
  With hir for to bee.
Bot it served hir of no thyng:
A preste he made forthe bryng,
Hym a messe for to syng,
  And aftir rode he.

Now fro tham gun he ryde;
Ther wiste no man that tyde
Whedirwarde he wolde ryde,
  His sorowes to amende.
Forthe he rydes allone;
Fro tham he wolde everichone:
Mighte no man with hym gone,
  Ne whedir he wolde lende.
Bot forthe thus rydes he ay,
The certen sothe als I yow say,
Till he come at a way
  By a wode-ende.
Then herde he faste hym by
Als it were a woman cry:
Scho prayed to mylde Mary

Som socoure hir to sende.

Scho sende hir socour full gude,
Mary, that es mylde of mode.
As he come thurgh the wode,
    A ferly he fande.
A birde, brighteste of ble,
Stode faste bonden till a tre -
I say it yow certanly -
    Bothe fote and hande.
Sone askede he who,
When he sawe hir tho,
That had served hir so,
    That lady in lande.
Scho said, "Sir, the Blake Knyghte
Solde be my lorde with righte;
He hase me thusgates dighte
    Here for to stande."

She says, "Here mon I stande
For a faute that he fande
That sall I warande
    Is my moste mone.
Now to the I sall say:
Appon my bedd I lay
Appon the laste Yole-day -
    Twelve monethes es gone -
Were he knyghte, were he king,
He come one his playnge.
With me he chaungede a ring,
    The richeste of one.
The body myght I noghte see

That made that chaungyng with me,
Bot what that ever he be,
   The better hase he tone!"

Scho says, "The better hase he tane;
Siche a vertue es in the stane,
In alle this werlde wote I nane
   Siche stone in a rynge;
A man that had it in were
One his body for to bere,
There scholde no dyntys hym dere,
   Ne to the dethe brynge."
And then wiste Sir Percevale
Full wele by the ladys tale
That he had broghte hir in bale
   Thurgh his chaungyng.
Than also sone sayd he
To that lady so fre,
"I sall the louse fro the tre,
   Als I ame trewe kyng."

He was bothe kyng and knyght:
Wele he helde that he highte;
He loused the lady so brighte,
   Stod bown to the tre.
Down satt the lady,
And yong Percevall hir by.
Forwaked was he wery:
   Rist hym wolde he.
He wende wele for to ryst,
Bot it wolde nothyng laste.
Als he lay althir best,

65

His hede one hir kne,
Scho putt on Percevell wighte,
Bad hym fle with all his myghte,
"For yonder comes the Blake Knyghte;
    Dede mon ye be!"

Scho sayd, "Dede mon ye be,
I say yow, sir certanly:
Yonder out comes he
    That will us bothe slee!"
The knyghte gan hir answere,
"Tolde ye me noghte lang ere
Ther solde no dynttis me dere,
    Ne wirke me no woo?"
The helme on his hede he sett;
Bot or he myght to his stede get,
The Blak Knyght with hym mett,
    His maistrys to mo.
He sayd, "How! hase thou here
Fonden now thi play-fere?
Ye schall haby it full dere
    Er that I hethen go!"

He said, "Or I hethyn go,
I sall sle yow bothe two,
And all siche othir mo,
    Thaire waryson to yelde."
Than sayd Percevell the fre,
"Now sone than sall we see
Who that es worthy to bee
    Slayne in the felde."
No more speke thay that tyde,

Bot sone togedir gan thay ryde,
Als men that wolde were habyde,
  With schafte and with schelde.
Than Sir Percevell the wight
Bare down the Blake Knyght.
Than was the lady so bright
  His best socour in telde;

Scho was the beste of his belde:
Bot scho had there bene his schelde,
He had bene slayne in the felde,
  Right certeyne in hy.
Ever als Percevell the kene
Sold the knyghtis bane hafe bene,
Ay went the lady bytwene
  And cryed, "Mercy!"
Than the lady he forbere,
And made the Blak Knyghte to swere
Of alle evylls that there were,
  Forgiffe the lady.
And Percevell made the same othe
That he come never undir clothe
To do that lady no lothe
  That pendid to velany.

"I did hir never no velany;
Bot slepande I saw hir ly:
Than kist I that lady -
  I will it never layne.
I tok a ryng that I fande;
I left hir, I undirstande,
That sall I wele warande,

67

Anothir ther-agayne."
Thofe it were for none other thyng,
He swere by Jhesu, Heven-kyng,
To wete withowtten lesyng,
 And here to be slayne;
"And all redy is the ryng;
And thou will myn agayne bryng,
Here will I make the chaungyng,
 And of myn awnn be fayne."

He saise, "Of myn I will be fayne."
The Blak Knyghte ansuers agayne:
Sayd, "For sothe, it is noghte to layne,
 Thou come over-late.
Als sone als I the ryng fande,
I toke it sone off hir hande;
To the lorde of this lande
 I bare it one a gate.
That gate with grefe hafe I gone:
I bare it to a gude mone,
The stalwortheste geant of one
 That any man wate.
Es it nowther knyghte ne kyng
That dorste aske hym that ryng,
That he ne wolde hym down dyng
 With harmes full hate."

"Be thay hate, be thay colde,"
Than said Percevell the bolde,
For the tale that he tolde
 He wex all tene.
He said, "Heghe on galous mote he hyng

That to the here giffes any ryng,
Bot thou myn agayne brynge,
   Thou haste awaye geven!
And yif it may no nother be,
Righte sone than tell thou me
The sothe: whilke that es he
   Thou knawes, that es so kene?
Ther es no more for to say,
Bot late me wynn it yif I may,
For thou hase giffen thi part of bothe away,
   Thof thay had better bene."

He says, "Thofe thay had better bene."
The knyghte ansuerde in tene,
"Thou sall wele wete, withowtten wene,
   Wiche that es he!
If thou dare do als thou says,
Sir Percevell de Galays,
In yone heghe palays,
   Therin solde he be,
The riche ryng with that grym!
The stane es bright and nothyng dym;
For sothe, ther sall thou fynd hym:
   I toke it fro me;
Owthir within or withowt,
Or one his play ther abowte,
Of the he giffes littill dowte,
   And that sall thou see."

He says, "That sall thou see,
I say the full sekirly."
And than forthe rydis he

Wondirly swythe.
The geant stode in his holde,
That had those londis in wolde:
Saw Percevell, that was bolde,
   One his lande dryfe;
He calde one his portere:
"How-gate may this fare?
I se a bolde man yare
   On my lande ryfe.
Go reche me my playlome,
And I sall go to hym sone;
Hym were better hafe bene at Rome,
   So ever mote I thryfe!"

Whethir he thryfe or he the,
Ane iryn clobe takes he;
Agayne Percevell the fre
   He went than full right.
The clobe wheyhed reghte wele
That a freke myght it fele:
The hede was of harde stele,
   Twelve stone weghte!
Ther was iryn in the wande,
Ten stone of the lande,
And one was byhynde his hande,
   For holdyng was dight.
Ther was thre and twenty in hale;
Full evyll myght any men smale,
That men telles nowe in tale,
   With siche a lome fighte.

Now are thay bothe bown,

Mett one a more brown,
A mile withowt any town,
   Boldly with schelde.
Than saide the geant so wight,
Als sone als he sawe the knyght,
"Mahown, loved be thi myght!"
   And Percevell byhelde.
"Art thou hym, that," saide he than,
"That slew Gollerothirame?
I had no brothir bot hym ane,
   When he was of elde."
Than said Percevell the fre,
"Thurgh grace of God so sall I the,
And siche geantes as ye
   Sle thaym in the felde!"

Siche metyng was seldom sene.
The dales dynned thaym bytwene
For dynttis that thay gaffe bydene
   When thay so mett.
The gyant with his clobe-lome
Wolde hafe strekyn Percevell sone,
Bot he therunder wightely come,
   A stroke hym to sett.
The geant missede of his dynt;
The clobe was harde as the flynt:
Or he myght his staffe stynt
   Or his strengh lett,
The clobe in the erthe stode:
To the midschafte it wode.
The Percevell the gode,
   Hys swerde owt he get.

By then hys swerde owt he get,
Strykes the geant withowtten lett,
Merkes even to his nekk,
    Reght even ther he stode;
His honde he strykes hym fro,
His lefte fote also,
With siche dyntis as tho.
    Nerre hym he yode.
Then sayd Percevell, "I undirstande
Thou myghte with a lesse wande
Hafe weledid better thi hande
    And hafe done the some gode;
Now bese it never for ane
The clobe of the erthe tane.
I tell thi gatis alle gane, 5
    Bi the gude Rode!"

He says, "By the gud Rode,
As evyll als thou ever yode,
Of thi fote thou getis no gode;
    Bot lepe if thou may!"
The geant gan the clobe lefe,
And to Percevell a dynt he yefe
In the nekk with his nefe.
    So ne neghede thay.
At that dynt was he tene:
He strikes off the hande als clene
Als ther hadde never none bene.
    That other was awaye.
Sythen his hede gan he off hafe;
He was ane unhende knave

A geantberde so to schafe,
  For sothe, als I say!

Now for sothe, als I say,
He lete hym ly there he lay,
And rydis forthe one his way
  To the heghe holde.
The portare saw his lorde slayne;
The kayes durste he noght layne.
He come Percevell agayne;
  The gatis he hym yolde.
At the firste bygynnyng,
He askede the portere of the ryng -
If he wiste of it any thyng -
  And he hym than tolde:
He taughte hym sone to the kiste
Ther he alle the golde wiste,
Bade hym take what hym liste
  Of that he hafe wolde.

Percevell sayde, hafe it he wolde,
And schott owtt all the golde
Righte there appon the faire molde;
  The ryng owte glade.
The portare stode besyde,
Sawe the ryng owt glyde,
Sayde ofte, "Wo worthe the tyde
That ever was it made!"
Percevell answerde in hy,
And asked wherefore and why
He banned it so brothely,
  Bot if he cause hade.

73

Then alsone said he,
And sware by his lewté:
"The cause sall I tell the,
   Withowten any bade."

He says, "Withowtten any bade,
The knyghte that it here hade,
Theroff a presande he made,
   And hedir he it broghte.
Mi mayster tuke it in his hande,
Ressayved faire that presande:
He was chefe lorde of this lande,
   Als man that mekill moghte.
That tyme was here fast by
Wonnande a lady,
And hir wele and lely
   He luffede, als me thoghte.
So it byfelle appon a day,
Now the sothe als I sall say,
Mi lorde went hym to play,
   And the lady bysoghte.

Now the lady byseches he
That scho wolde his leman be;
Fast he frayned that free,
   For any kyns aughte.
At the firste bygynnyng,
He wolde hafe gyffen hir the ryng;
And when scho sawe the tokynyng,
   Then was scho un-saughte.
Scho gret and cried in hir mone;
Sayd, 'Thefe, hase thou my sone slone

And the ryng fro hym tone,
  That I hym bitaughte?'
Hir clothes ther scho rafe hir fro,
And to the wodd gan scho go;
Thus es the lady so wo,
  And this is the draghte.

For siche draghtis als this,
Now es the lady wode, iwys,
And wilde in the wodde scho es,
  Ay sythen that ilke tyde.
Fayne wolde I take that free,
Bot alsone als scho sees me,
Faste awaye dose scho flee:
  Will scho noghte abyde."
Then sayde Sir Percevell,
"I will assaye full snelle
To make that lady to duelle;
  Bot I will noghte ryde:
One my fete will I ga,
That faire lady to ta.
Me aughte to bryng hir of wa:
  I laye in hir syde."

He sayse, "I laye in hir syde;
I sall never one horse ryde
Till I hafe sene hir in tyde,
  Spede if I may;
Ne none armoure that may be
Sall come appone me
Till I my modir may see,
  Be nyghte or by day.

Bot reghte in the same wode
That I firste fro hir yode,
That sall be in my mode
    Aftir myn other play;
Ne I ne sall never mare
Come owt of yone holtis hare
Till I wete how scho fare,
    For sothe, als I saye."

Now for sothe, als I say,
With that he helde one his way,
And one the morne, when it was day,
    Forthe gonn he fare.
His armour he leved therin,
Toke one hym a gayt-skynne,
And to the wodde gan he wyn,
    Among the holtis hare.
A sevenyght long hase he soghte;
His modir ne fyndis he noghte.
Of mete ne drynke he ne roghte,
    So full he was of care.
Till the nynte day, byfell
That he come to a welle
Ther he was wonte for to duelle
    And drynk take hym thare.

When he had dronken that tyde,
Forthirmare gan he glyde;
Than was he warre, hym besyde,
    Of the lady so fre;
Bot when scho sawe hym thare,
Scho bygan for to dare,

76

And sone gaffe hym answare,
  That brighte was of ble.
Scho bigan to call and cry:
Sayd, "Siche a sone hade I!"
His hert lightened in hy,
  Blythe for to bee.
Be that he come hir nere
That scho myght hym here,
He said, "My modir full dere,
  Wele byde ye me!"

Be that, so nere getis he
That scho myghte nangatis fle,
I say yow full certeynly.
  Hir byhoved ther to byde.
Scho stertis appon hym in tene;
Wete ye wele, withowtten wene,
Had hir myghte so mekill bene,
  Scho had hym slayne that tyde!
Bot his myghte was the mare,
And up he toke his modir thare;
One his bake he hir bare:
  Pure was his pryde.
To the castell, withowtten mare,
The righte way gon he fare;
The portare was redy yare,
  And lete hym in glyde.

In with his modir he glade,
Als he sayse that it made;
With siche clothes als thay hade,

Thay happed hir forthy.
The geant had a drynk wroghte,
The portere sone it forthe broghte,
For no man was his thoghte
   Bot for that lady.
Thay wolde not lett long thon,
Bot lavede in hir with a spone.
Then scho one slepe fell also sone,
   Reght certeyne in hy.
Thus the lady there lyes
Thre nyghttis and thre dayes,
And the portere alwayes
   Lay wakande hir by.

Thus the portare woke hir by -
Ther whills hir luffed sekerly, -
Till at the laste the lady
   Wakede, als I wene.
Then scho was in hir awenn state
And als wele in hir gate
Als scho hadde nowthir arely ne late
   Never therowte bene.
Thay sett tham down one thaire kne,
Thanked Godde, alle three,
That he wolde so appon tham see
   As it was there sene.
Sythen aftir gan thay ta
A riche bathe for to ma,
And made the lady in to ga,
   In graye and in grene.

Than Sir Percevell in hy

Toke his modir hym by,
I say yow than certenly,
  And home went hee.
Grete lordes and the Qwene
Welcomed hym al bydene;
When thay hym on lyfe sene;
  Than blythe myghte thay bee.
Sythen he went into the Holy Londe,
Wanne many cités full stronge,
And there was he slayne, I undirstonde;
  Thusgatis endis hee.
Now Jhesu Criste, hevens Kyng,
Als He es Lorde of all thyng,
Grante us all His blyssyng!
  Amen, for charyté!

Quod Robert Thornton
Explicit Sir Percevell de Gales
Here endys the Romance of Sir Percevell of Gales, Cosyn to King
Arthoure.

YWAIN AND GAWAIN

Here bigyns Ywain and Gawain

Almyghti God that made mankyn,
He schilde His servandes out of syn
And mayntene tham with myght and mayne
That herkens Ywayne and Gawayne;
Thai war knightes of the Tabyl Rownde,
Tharfore listens a lytel stownde.
   Arthure, the Kyng of Yngland,
That wan al Wales with his hand
And al Scotland, als sayes the buke,
And mani mo, if men wil luke,
Of al knightes he bare the pryse.
In werld was none so war ne wise.
Trew he was in alkyn thing.
Als it byfel to swilk a kyng,
He made a feste, the soth to say,
Opon the Witsononday
At Kerdyf that es in Wales.
And efter mete thare in the hales
Ful grete and gay was the assemblé
Of lordes and ladies of that cuntré,
And als of kynghtes war and wyse
And damisels of mykel pryse.
Ilkane with other made grete gamin
And grete solace als thai war samin.
Fast thai carped and curtaysly
Of dedes of armes and of veneri
And of gude knightes that lyfed then,
And how men might tham kyndeli ken
By doghtines of thaire gude dede

On ilka syde, wharesum thai yede -
For thai war stif in ilka stowre.
And tharfore gat thai grete honowre.
Thai tald of more trewth tham bitwene
Than now omang men here es sene,
For trowth and luf es al bylaft;
Men uses now another craft.
With worde men makes it trew and stabil,
Bot in thaire faith es noght bot fabil;
With the mowth men makes it hale,
Bot trew trowth es nane in the tale.
Tharfore hereof now wil I blyn,
Of the Kyng Arthure I wil bygin
And of his curtayse cumpany;
Thare was the flowre of chevallry.
Swilk lose thai wan with speres-horde
Over al the werld went the worde.

   After mete went the Kyng
Into chamber to slepeing,
And also went with him the Quene.
That byheld thai al bydene,
For thai saw tham never so
On high dayes to chamber go.
Bot sone, when thai war went to slepe,
Knyghtes sat the dor to kepe:
Sir Dedyne and Sir Segramore,
Sir Gawayn and Sir Kay sat thore,
And also sat thare Sir Ywaine
And Colgrevance of mekyl mayn.
This knight that hight Colgrevance,
Tald his felows of a chance
And of a stowre he had in bene,

And al his tale herd the Quene.
The chamber dore sho has unshet,
And down omang tham scho hir set;
Sodainli sho sat down right,
Or ani of tham of hir had sight
Bot Colgrevance rase up in hy,
And thareof had Syr Kay envy,
For he was of his tong a skalde,
And forto boste was he ful balde.
"Ow, Colgrevance," said Sir Kay,
"Ful light of lepes has thou bene ay.
Thou wenes now that the sal fall
Forto be hendest of us all.
And the Quene sal understand,
That here es none so unkunand
Al if thou rase and we sat styll.
We ne dyd it for none yll,
Ne for no manere of fayntise,
Ne us denyd noght forto rise,
That we ne had resen had we hyr sene."
"Sir Kay, I wote wele," sayd the Quene,
"And it war gude thou left swilk sawes
And noght despise so thi felawes."
"Madame," he said, "by Goddes dome,
We ne wist no thing of thi come
And if we did noght curtaysly,
Takes to no velany.
Bot pray ye now this gentil man
To tel the tale that he bygan."
Colgrevance said to Sir Kay:
"Bi grete God that aw this day,
Na mare manes me thi flyt

Than it war a flies byt.
Ful oft wele better men than I
Has thou desspised desspytusely.
It es ful semeli, als me think,
A brok omang men forto stynk.
So it fars by the, Syr Kay:
Of weked wordes has thou bene ay.
And, sen thi wordes er wikked and fell,
This time tharto na more I tell,
Bot of the thing that I bygan."
And sone Sir Kay him answerd than
And said ful tite unto the Quene:
"Madame, if ye had noght here bene,
We sold have herd a selly case;
Now let ye us of oure solace.
Tharfore, madame, we wald yow pray,
That ye cumand him to say
And tel forth, als he had tyght."
Than answerd that hende knight:
"Mi lady es so avyse,
That scho wil noght cumand me
To tel that towches me to ill;
Scho es noght of so weked will."
Sir Kai said than ful smertli:
"Madame, al hale this cumpani
Praies yow hertly now omell,
That he his tale forth might tell.
If ye wil noght for oure praying,
For faith ye aw unto the kyng,
Cumandes him his tale to tell,
That we mai here how it byfell."
Than said the Quene, "Sir Colgrevance,

I prai the tak to no grevance
This kene karping of Syr Kay;
Of weked wordes has he bene ay,
So that none may him chastise.
Tharfore I prai the, on al wise,
That thou let noght for his sawes,
At tel to me and thi felawes
Al thi tale, how it bytid.
For my luf I the pray and byd."

  "Sertes, madame, that es me lath
Bot for I wil noght mak yow wrath,
Yowre cumandment I sal fulfill,
If ye wil listen me untill,
With hertes and eres understandes;
And I sal tel yow swilk tithandes,
That ye herd never none slike
Reherced in no kynges ryke.
Bot word fares als dose the wind,
Bot if men it in hert bynd;
And, wordes wo so trewly tase,
By the eres into the hert it gase,
And in the hert thare es the horde
And knawing of ilk mans worde.

  "Herkens, hende unto my spell.
Trofels sal I yow nane tell,
Ne lesinges forto ger yow lagh,
Bot I sal say right als I sagh.
Now als this time sex yere
I rade allane, als ye sal here,
Obout forto seke aventurs,
Wele armid in gude armurs.
In a frith I fand a strete;

Ful thik and hard, I you bihete,
With thornes, breres, and moni a quyn.
Nerehand al day I rade thareyn,
And thurgh I past with mekyl payn.
Than come I sone into a playn,
Whare I gan se a bretise brade,
And thederward ful fast I rade.
I saw the walles and the dyke,
And hertly wele it gan me lyke;
And on the drawbrig saw I stand
A knight with fawkon on his hand.
This ilk knight, that be ye balde,
Was lord and keper of that halde.
I hailsed him kindly als I kowth;
He answerd me mildeli with mowth.
Mi sterap toke that hende knight
And kindly cumanded me to lyght;
His cumandment I did onane,
And into hall sone war we tane.
He thanked God, that gude man,
Sevyn sithes or ever he blan,
And the way that me theder broght,
And als the aventurs that I soght.
   "Thus went we in, God do him mede,
And in his hand he led my stede.
When we are in that fayre palays -
It was ful worthly wroght always -
I saw no man of moder born.
Bot a burde hang us biforn,
Was nowther of yren ne of tre,
Ne I ne wist whareof it might be.
And by that bord hang a mall.

The knyght smate on tharwithal
Thrise, and by then might men se
Bifore him come a faire menye,
Curtayse men in worde and dede.
To stabil sone thai led mi stede.
   "A damisel come unto me,
The semeliest that ever I se,
Lufsumer lifed never in land.
Hendly scho toke me by the hand,
And sone that gentyl creature
Al unlaced myne armure.
Into a chamber sho me led,
And with a mantil scho me cled:
It was of purpure faire and fine
And the pane of riche ermyne.
Al the folk war went us fra,
And thare was none than bot we twa.
Scho served me hendely to hend:
Hir maners might no man amend.
Of tong sho was trew and renable
And of hir semblant soft and stabile.
Ful fain I wald, if that I might,
Have woned with that swete wight.
And, when we sold go to sopere,
That lady with a lufsom chere
Led me down into the hall.
Thare war we served wele at all;
It nedes noght to tel the mese,
For wonder wele war we at esse.
Byfor me sat the lady bright
Curtaisly my mete to dyght;
Us wanted nowther baken ne roste.

And efter soper sayd myne oste
That he cowth noght tel the day
That ani knight are with him lay,
Or that ani aventures soght.
Tharfore he prayed me, if I moght,
On al wise, when I come ogayne,
That I sold cum to him sertayne.
I said, "Sir, gladly, yf I may."
It had bene shame have said him nay.
    "That night had I ful gude rest
And mi stede esed of the best.
Alsone als it was dayes lyght,
Forth to fare sone was I dyght.
Mi leve of mine ost toke I thare
And went mi way withowten mare,
Aventures forto layt in land.
A faire forest sone I fand.
Me thoght mi hap thare fel ful hard,
For thare was mani a wilde lebard,
Lions, beres, bath bul and bare,
That rewfully gan rope and rare.
Oway I drogh me, and with that
I saw sone whare a man sat
On a lawnd, the fowlest wight
That ever yit man saw in syght.
He was a lathly creature,
For fowl he was out of mesure;
A wonder mace in hand he hade,
And sone mi way to him I made.
His hevyd, me thoght, was als grete
Als of a rowncy or a nete;
Unto his belt hang his hare,

And efter that byheld I mare.
To his forhede byheld I than,
Was bradder than twa large span;
He had eres als ane olyfant
And was wele more than geant.
His face was ful brade and flat;
His nese was cutted als a cat;
His browes war like litel buskes;
And his tethe like bare tuskes.
A ful grete bulge opon his bak -
Thare was noght made withowten lac.
His chin was fast until his brest;
On his mace he gan him rest.
Also it was a wonder wede,
That the cherle yn gede;
Nowther of wol ne of line
Was the wede that he went yn.
   "When he me sagh, he stode upright.
I frayned him if he wolde fight,
For tharto was I in gude will,
Bot als a beste than stode he still.
I hopid that he no wittes kowth,
No reson forto speke with mowth.
To him I spak ful hardily
And said, 'What ertow, belamy?'
He said ogain, 'I am a man.'
I said, 'Swilk saw I never nane.
What ertow?' alsone said he.
I said, 'Swilk als thou here may se.'
I said, 'What does thou here allane?'
He said, 'I kepe thir bestes ilkane.'
I said, 'That es mervaile, think me,

91

For I herd never of man bot the
In wildernes ne in forestes,
That kepeing had of wilde bestes,
Bot thai war bunden fast in halde.'
He sayd, 'Of thire es none so balde
Nowther by day ne bi night
Anes to pas out of mi sight.'
I sayd, 'How so? Tel me thi scill.'
'Parfay,' he said, 'gladly I will.'
He said, 'In al this faire foreste
Es thare none so wilde beste,
That remu dar, bot stil stand,
When I am to him cumand.
Any ay, when that I wil him fang
With mi fingers that er strang,
I ger him cri on swilk manere,
That al the bestes when thai him here,
Obout me than cum thai all,
And to mi fete fast thai fall,
On thaire manere merci to cry.
Bot understand now redyli,
Olyve es thare lifand no ma
Bot I that durst omang tham ga,
That he ne sold sone be al torent.
Bot thai er at my comandment;
To me thai cum when I tham call,
And I am maister of tham all.'

  "Than he asked onone right,
What man I was. I said, 'A knyght
That soght aventurs in that land,
My body to asai and fande.
And I the pray of thi kownsayle,

Thou teche me to sum mervayle.'
He sayd, 'I can no wonders tell,
Bot here bisyde es a well.
Wend theder and do als I say;
Thou passes noght al quite oway.
Folow forth this ilk strete,
And sone sum mervayles sal thou mete.
The well es under the fairest tre
That ever was in this cuntré;
By that well hinges a bacyne
That es of gold gude and fyne,
With a cheyne, trewly to tell,
That wil reche into the well.
Thare es a chapel nere tharby,
That nobil es and ful lufely.
By the well standes a stane;
Tak the bacyn sone onane
And cast on water with thi hand,
And sone thou sal se new tithand.
A storme sal rise and a tempest
Al obout, by est and west;
Thou sal here mani thonor-blast
Al obout the blawand fast.
And thare sal cum slik slete and rayne
That unnese sal thou stand ogayne;
Of lightnes sal thou se a lowe,
Unnethes thou sal thi selven knowe.
And if thou pas withowten grevance,
Than has thou the fairest chance,
That ever yit had any knyght,
That theder come to kyth his myght.'
  "Than toke I leve and went my way

And rade unto the midday.
By than I come whare I sold be,
I saw the chapel and the tre.
Thare I fand the fayrest thorne
That ever groued sen God was born.
So thik it was with leves grene,
Might no rayn cum tharbytwene;
And that grenes lastes ay,
For no winter dere yt may.
I fand the bacyn als he talde,
And the wel with water kalde.
An amerawd was the stane -
Richer saw I never nane -
On fowre rubyes on heght standand.
Thaire light lasted over al the land,
And when I saw that semely syght,
It made me bath joyful and lyght.
I toke the bacyn sone onane
And helt water opon the stane.
The weder wex than wonder-blak,
And the thoner fast gan crak.
Thare come slike stormes of hayl and rayn,
Unnethes I might stand thare ogayn;
The store windes blew ful lowd,
So kene come never are of clowd.
I was drevyn with snaw and slete,
Unnethes I might stand on my fete.
In my face the levening smate,
I wend have brent, so was it hate,
That weder made me so will of rede,
I hopid sone to have my dede;
And sertes, if it lang had last,

I hope I had never thethin past.
Bot thorgh His might that tholed wownd,
The storme sesed within a stownde.
Than wex the weder fayre ogayne,
And thareof was I wonder-fayne;
For best comforth of al thing
Es solace efter myslikeing.
   "Than saw I sone a mery syght:
Of al the fowles that er in flyght,
Lighted so thik opon that tre,
That bogh ne lefe none might I se.
So merily than gon thai sing,
That al the wode bigan to ring;
Ful mery was the melody
Of thaire sang and of thaire cry.
Thare herd never man none swilk,
Bot if ani had herd that ilk.
And when that mery dyn was done,
Another noyse than herd I sone,
Als it war of horsmen
Mo than owther nyen or ten.
   "Sone than saw I cum a knyght;
In riche armurs was he dight,
And sone, when I gan on him loke,
Mi shelde and spere to me I toke.
That knight to me hied ful fast,
And kene wordes out gan he cast.
He bad that I sold tel him tite,
Whi I did him swilk despite,
With weders wakened him of rest
And done him wrang in his forest.
'Tharfore,' he said, 'thou sal aby!'

And with that come he egerly
And said I had ogayn resowne
Done him grete destrucciowne,
And might it never more amend.
Tharfore he bad I sold me fend.
And sone I smate him on the shelde,
Mi schaft brac out in the felde,
And than he bare me sone bi strenkith
Out of my sadel my speres lenkith.
I wate that he was largely
By the shuldres mare than I;
And bi the ded that I sal thole,
Mi stede by his was bot a fole.
For mate I lay down on the grownde,
So was I stonayd in that stownde.
A worde to me wald he noght say,
Bot toke my stede and went his way.
Ful sarily than thare I sat,
For wa I wist noght what was what.
With my stede he went in hy
The same way that he come by.
And I durst folow him no ferr
For dout me solde bitide werr.
And also yit, by Goddes dome,
I ne wist whare he bycome.
    "Than I thoght how I had hight
Unto myne ost, the hende knyght,
And also til his lady bryght,
To com ogayn if that I myght.
Mine armurs left I thare ilkane,
For els myght I noght have gane.
Unto myne in I come by day.

The hende knight and the fayre may
Of my come war thai ful glade,
And nobil semblant thai me made.
In al thinges thai have tham born
Als thai did the night biforn.
Sone thai wist whare I had bene,
And said that thai had never sene
Knyght that ever theder come,
Take the way ogayn home.
On this wise that tyme I wroght;
I fand the folies that I soght."

    "Now sekerly," said Sir Ywayne,
"Thou ert my cosyn jermayne;
Trew luf suld be us bytwene,
Als sold bytwyx brether bene.
Thou ert a fole at thou ne had are
Tald me of this ferly fare,
For sertes I sold onone ryght
Have venged the of that ilk knyght.
So sal I yit, if that I may."

    And than als smertly sayed Syr Kay -
He karpet to tham wordes grete:
"It es sene, now es efter mete,
Mare boste es in a pot of wyne
Than in a karcas of Saynt Martyne.
Arme the smertly, Syr Ywayne,
And sone that thou war cumen ogayne;
Luke thou fil wele thi panele,
And in thi sadel set the wele.
And when thou wendes, I the pray,
Thi baner wele that thou desplay;
And, rede I, or thou wende,

Thou tak thi leve at ilka frende.
And if it so bytide this nyght,
That the in slepe dreche ani wight
Or any dremis mak the rad,
Turn ogayn and say I bad."
    The quene answerd with milde mode
And said, "Sir Kay, ertow wode?
What the devyl es the withyn,
At thi tong may never blyn
Thi felows so fowly to shende?
Sertes, Sir Kay, thou ert unhende.
By Him that for us sufferd pine,
Syr, and thi tong war myne
I sold bical it tyte of treson,
And so might thou do, by gude reson.
Thi tong dose the grete dishonowre,
And tharefore es it thi traytowre."
And than alsone Syr Ywayne
Ful hendly answerd ogayne,
Al if men sayd hym velany,
He karped ay ful curtaysly:
"Madame," he said unto the quene,
"Thare sold na stryf be us bytwene.
Unkowth men wele may he shende
That to his felows es so unhende.
And als, madame, men says sertayne
That, wo so flites or turnes ogayne,
He bygins al the melle:
So wil I noght it far by me.
Lates him say haley his thoght;
His wordes greves me right noght."
    Als thai war in this spekeing

Out of the chamber come the kyng.
The barons that war thare, sertayn,
Smertly rase thai him ogayne.
He bad tham sit down al bydene,
And down he set him by the quene.
The quene talde him fayre and wele,
Als sho kowth, everilka dele
Ful apertly al the chance
Als it bifel Syr Colgrevance.
When sho had talde him how it ferd,
And the king hyr tale had herd,
He sware by his owyn crowne
And his fader sowl Uter Pendragowne,
That he sold se that ilk syght
By that day thethin a fowretenight,
On Saint Johns evyn, the Baptist,
That best barn was under Crist.
"Swith," he sayd, "wendes with me,
Who so wil that wonder se."
    The kynges word might noght be hid,
Over al the cowrt sone was it kyd;
And thare was none so litel page
That he ne was fayn of that vayage;
And knyghtes and swiers war ful fayne;
Mysliked none bot Syr Ywayne.
To himself he made grete mane,
For he wald have went allane.
In hert he had grete myslykyng
For the wending of the kyng,
Al for he hopid, withowten fayle,
That Sir Kay sold ask the batayle,
Or els Sir Gawayn, knyght vailant;

99

And owther wald the king grant.
Who so it wald first crave
Of tham two, sone might it have.
   The kynges wil wald he noght bide,
Worth of him, what may bityde;
Bi him allane he thoght to wend
And tak the grace that God wald send.
He thoght to be wele on hys way,
Or it war passed the thryd day,
And to asay if he myght mete
With that ilk narow strete
With thornes and with breres set,
That mens way might lightli let,
And also forto fynd the halde,
That Sir Colgrevance of talde.
The knyght and the mayden meke,
The forest fast than wald he seke,
And als the karl of Kaymes kyn
And the wilde bestes with him,
The tre with briddes thare opon,
The chapel, the bacyn, and the stone.
His thoght wald he tel to no frende,
Until he wyst how it wald ende.
Than went Ywaine to his yn;
His men he fand redy thareyn.
Unto a swier gan he say,
"Go swith and sadel my palfray,
And so thou do my strang stede,
And tak with the my best wede.
At yone gate I wil outryde;
Withowten town I sal the bide.
And hy the smertly unto me,

For I most make a jorné.
Ogain sal thou bring my palfra,
And forbede the oght to say.
If thou wil any more me se,
Lat none wit of my preveté;
And if ani man the oght frayn,
Luke now lely that thou layn."
"Sir," he said, "with ful gude will,
Als ye byd, I sal fulfyll.
At yowre awyn wil may ye ride,
For me ye sal noght be ascryed."
    Forth than went Sir Ywayne;
He thinkes, or he cum ogayne,
To wreke his kosyn at his myght.
The squier has his hernays dyght;
He did right als his mayster red;
His stede, his armurs he him led.
When Ywayn was withowten town,
Of his palfray lighted he down
And dight him right wele in his wede
And lepe up on his gude stede.
Furth he rade onone right,
Until it neghed nere the nyght.
He passed many high mowntayne
In wildernes and mony a playne,
Til he come to that lethir sty,
That him byhoved pass by.
Than was he seker for to se
The wel and the fayre tre.
The chapel saw he at the last,
And theder hyed he ful fast.
More curtaysi and more honowre

Fand he with tham in that toure,
And mare conforth by monyfalde,
Than Colgrevance had him of talde.
That night was he herberd thare:
So wele was he never are.

   At morn he went forth by the strete,
And with the cherel sone gan he mete
That sold tel to him the way.
He sayned him, the soth to say,
Twenty sith or ever he blan;
Swilk mervayle had he of that man;
For he had wonder that nature
Myght mak so fowl a creature.
Than to the well he rade gude pase,
And doun he lighted in that place;
And sone the bacyn has he tane
And kest water opon the stane;
And sone thare wex withowten fayle,
Wind and thonor and rayn and haile.
When it was sesed, than saw he
The fowles light opon the tre;
Thai sang ful fayre opon that thorn,
Right als thai had done byforn.

   And sone he saw cumand a knight
Als fast so the fowl in flyght
With rude sembland and sterne chere,
And hastily he neghed nere.
To speke of lufe na time was thare,
For aither hated uther ful sare.
Togeder smertly gan thai drive,
Thaire sheldes sone bigan to ryve,
Thaire shaftes cheverd to thaire hand,

Bot thai war bath ful wele syttand.
Out thai drogh thaire swerdes kene
And delt strakes tham bytwene;
Al to peces thai hewed thaire sheldes,
The culpons flegh out in the feldes.
On helmes strake thay so with yre,
At ilka strake outbrast the fyre.
Aither of tham gude buffettes bede,
And nowther wald styr of the stede.
Ful kenely thai kyd thaire myght
And feyned tham noght forto fight.
On thaire hauberkes that men myght ken,
The blode out of thaire bodyes ren;
Aither on other laid so fast,
The batayl might noght lang last.
Hauberkes er broken and helmes reven,
Stif strakes war thare gyfen;
Thai faght on hors stifly always;
The batel was wele more to prays.
Bot at the last Syr Ywayne
On his felow kyd his mayne:
So egerly he smate him than,
He clefe the helme and the hernpan.
The knyght wist he was nere ded;
To fle than was his best rede,
And fast he fled with al hys mayne,
And fast folowd Syr Ywayne.
Bot he ne might him overtake,
Tharfore grete murning gan he make.
He folowd him ful stowtlyk
And wald have tane him ded or quik.
He folowd him to the ceté;

103

Na man lyfand met he.
When thai come to the kastel gate,
In he folowd fast thareate.
At aither entré was, iwys,
Straytly wroght a portculis
Shod wele with yren and stele
And also grunden wonder wele.
Under that than was a swyke,
That made Syr Ywain to myslike.
His hors fote toched thareon
Than fel the portculis onone
Bytwyx him and his hinder arsown.
Thorgh sadel and stede it smate al down,
His spores of his heles it schare;
Than had Ywaine murnyng mare.
Bot so he wend have passed quite,
Than fel the tother bifore als tyte.
A faire grace yit fel him swa,
Al if it smate his hors in twa
And his spors of aither hele,
That himself passed so wele.
   Bytwene tha gates now es he tane;
Tharfore he mase ful mukel mane,
And mikel murnyng gan he ma,
For the knyght was went him fra.
Als he was stoken in that stall,
He herd byhind him in a wall
A dore opend faire and wele,
And thareout come a damysel.
Efter hir the dore sho stak,
Ful hinde wordes to him sho spak.
"Syr," sho said, "by Saint Myghell,

Here thou has a febil ostell.
Thou mon be ded, es noght at laine,
For my lord that thou has slayne.
Seker it es that thou him slogh;
My lady makes sorow ynogh
And al his menye everilkane.
Here has thou famen many ane
To be thi bane er thai ful balde.
Thou brekes noght out of this halde.
And, for thai wate thai may noght fayl,
Thai wil the sla in playn batayl."
He sayd, "Thai ne sal, so God me rede.
For al thaire might do me to dede,
Ne no handes opon me lay."
Sho said, "Na, sertes, if that I may!
Al if thou be here straytly stad,
Me think thou ert noght ful adrad.
And sir," sho said, "on al wise
I aw the honore and servyse.
I was in message at the king
Bifore this time, whils I was ying;
I was noght than savese,
Als a damysel aght to be.
Fro the tyme that I was lyght
In cowrt was none so hend knyght,
That unto me than walde take hede,
Bot thou allane, God do the mede.
Grete honore thou did to me,
And that sal I now quite the.
I wate, if thou be seldom sene,
Thou ert the Kyng son Uriene,
And thi name es Sir Ywayne.

Of me may thou be sertayne.
If thou wil my kownsail leve,
Thou sal find na man the to greve;
I sal lene the here mi ring,
Bot yelde it me at myne askyng.
When thou ert broght of al thi payn,
Yelde it than to me ogayne.
Als the bark hilles the tre,
Right so sal my ring do the;
When thou in hand has the stane,
Dere sal thai do the nane;
For the stane es of swilk myght,
Of the sal men have na syght."
   Wit ye wele that Sir Ywayne
Of thir wordes was ful fayne.
In at the dore sho him led
And did him sit opon hir bed.
A quylt ful nobil lay thareon,
Richer saw he never none.
Sho said if he wald any thing,
He sold be served at his liking.
He said that ete wald he fayn.
Sho went and come ful sone ogain;
A capon rosted broght sho sone,
A clene klath and brede tharone
And a pot with riche wine
And a pece to fil it yne.
He ete and drank with ful gude chere,
For tharof had he grete mystere.
When he had eten and dronken wele,
Grete noyse he herd in the kastele.
Thai soght overal him to have slayn,

To venge thaire lorde war thai ful bayn
Or that the cors in erth was layd.
The damysel sone to him sayd,
"Now seke thai the fast forto sla,
Bot whosoever com or ga,
Be thou never the more adred,
Ne styr thou noght out of this stede;
In this here seke thai wyll,
Bot on this bed luke thou be styll,
Of tham al mak thou na force.
Bot when that thai sal bere the cors
Unto the kyrk for to bery,
Than sal thou here a sary cry;
So sal thai mak a doleful dyn.
Than wil thay seke the eft herein;
Bot loke thou be of hert lyght,
For of the sal thai have no syght.
Here sal thou be, mawgré thaire berd,
And tharfore be thou noght aferd.
Thi famen sal be als the blynd,
Both byfor the and byhind,
On ilka side sal thou be soght.
Now most I ga, bot drede the noght,
For I sal do that the es lefe,
If al it turn me to mischefe."
   When sho come unto the gate,
Ful many men fand sho tharate
Wele armed, and wald ful fayn
Have taken and slane Sir Ywaine.
Half his stede thare fand thai
That within the gates lay;
Bot the knight thare fand thai noght:

Than was thare mekil sorow unsoght.
Dore ne window was thare nane,
Whare he myght oway gane.
Thai said he sold thare be laft,
Or els he cowth of wechecraft,
Or he cowth of nygromancy,
Or he had wenges forto fly.
Hastily than went thai all
And soght him in the maydens hall,
In chambers high (es noght at hide),
And in solers on ilka side.
Sir Ywaine saw ful wele al that,
And still opon the bed he sat.
Thare was nane that anes mynt
Unto the bed at smyte a dynt;
Al obout thai smate so fast,
That mani of thaire wapins brast.
Mekyl sorow thai made ilkane,
For thai ne myght wreke thaire lord bane.
Thai went oway with dreri chere,
And sone thare efter come the bere.
A lady folowd white so mylk,
In al that land was none swilk;
Sho wrang hir fingers, outbrast the blode.
For mekyl wa sho was nere wode.
Hir fayre hare scho al todrogh,
And ful oft fel sho down in swogh;
Sho wepe with a ful dreri voice.
The hali water and the Croyce
Was born bifore the procession;
Thare folowd mani a moder son;
Bifore the cors rade a knyght

On his stede that was ful wight,
In his armurs wele arayd,
With spere and target gudely grayd.
Than Sir Ywayn herd the cry
And the dole of that fayre lady;
For more sorow myght nane have,
Than sho had when he went to grave.
Prestes and monkes on thaire wyse
Ful solempnly did the servyse.
Als Lunet thare stode in the thrang,
Until Sir Ywaine thoght hir lang.
Out of the thrang the wai sho tase,
Unto Sir Ywaine fast sho gase.
Sho said, "Sir, how ertow stad?
I hope ful wele thou has bene rad."
"Sertes," he said, "thou sais wele thare;
So abayst was I never are."
He said, "Leman, I pray the,
If it any wise may be,
That I might luke a litel throw
Out at sum hole or sum window,
For wonder fayn," he sayd, "wald I
Have a sight of the lady."
The maiden than ful sone unshet
In a place a prevé weket.
Thare of the lady he had a syght.
Lowd sho cried to God almyght,
"Of his sins do hym pardowne,
For sertanly in no regyowne
Was never knight of his bewté,
Ne efter him sal never nane be;
In al the werld fro end to ende

Es none so curtayse ne so hende.
God grant the grace thou mai won
In hevyn with His owyn son;
For so large lifes none in lede
Ne none so doghty of gude dede."
When sho had thus made hir spell,
In swownyng ful oft sithes sho fell.
   Now lat we the lady be,
And of Sir Ywaine speke we.
Luf, that es so mekil of mayne,
Sare had wownded Sir Ywayne,
That whareso he sal ride or ga,
His hert sho has that es his fa. I
His hert he has set al bydene,
Whare himself dar noght be sene.
Bot thus in langing bides he
And hopes that it sal better be.
Al that war at the enterement,
Toke thaire leve at the lady gent,
And hame now er thai halely gane;
And the lady left allane
Dweland with hir chamberere
And other mo that war hir dere.
Than bigan hir noyes al new,
For sorow failed hir hide and hew.
Unto his sawl was sho ful hulde;
Opon a sawter al of gulde
To say the salmes fast sho bigan
And toke no tent unto no man.
   Than had Sir Ywain mekyl drede,
For he hoped noght to spede;
He said, "I am mekil to blame,

That I luf tham that wald me shame.
Bot yit I wite hir al with wogh,
Sen that I hir lord slogh.
I can noght se by nakyn gyn,
How that I hir luf sold wyn.
That lady es ful gent and small,
Hir yghen clere als es cristall;
Sertes thare es no man olive,
That kowth hir bewtese wele descrive."
   Thus was Syr Ywayne sted that sesowne;
He wroght ful mekyl ogayns resowne
To set his luf in swilk a stede,
Whare thai hated him to the dede.
He sayd he sold have hir to wive,
Or els he sold lose his lyve.
Thus als he in stody sat,
The mayden come to him with that.
Sho sayd, "How hasto farn this day,
Sen that I went fro the oway?"
Sone sho saw him pale and wan,
Sho wist wele what him ayled than.
Sho said, "I wote thi hert es set,
And sertes I ne sal noght it let;
Bot I sal help the fra presowne
And bring the to thi warisowne."
He said, "Sertes, damysele,
Out of this place wil I noght stele;
Bot I wil wende by dayes lyght,
That men may of me have sight
Opinly on ilka syde.
Worth of me what so bityde,
Manly wil I hethin wende."

Than answerd tha mayden hende,
"Sir, thow sal wend with honowre,
For thou sal have ful gude socowre.
Bot, sir, thou sal be here sertayne
A while unto I cum ogayne."
　　Sho kend al trewly his entent,
And tharfore es sho wightly went
Unto the lady faire and bright,
For unto hir right wele sho myght
Say whatsom hyr willes es.
For sho was al hir maystres,
Her keper, and hir cownsaylere.
To hir sho said, als ye sal here,
Bytwix tham twa in gude cownsayl,
"Madame," sho sayd, "I have mervayl
That ye sorow thus ever on ane.
For Goddes luf, lat be yowre mane.
Ye sold think over alkyn thyng
Of the Kinges Arthurgh cumyng.
Menes yow noght of the message
Of the Damysel Savage,
That in hir lettre to yow send?
Allas, who sal yow now defend
Yowre land and al that es thareyn,
Sen ye wil never of wepeing blyn?
A, madame, takes tent to me.
Ye ne have na knyght in this cuntré,
That durst right now his body bede
Forto do a doghty dede,
Ne forto bide the mekil boste
Of King Arthurgh and of his oste;
And if he find none hym ogayn,

Yowre landes er lorn, this es sertayn."
 The lady understode ful wele,
How sho hyr cownsaild ilka dele;
Sho bad hyr go hir way smertly,
And that sho war na more hardy
Swilk wordes to hyr at speke;
For wa hir hert wold al tobreke.
Sho bad, "Go wightly hethin oway."
Than the maiden thus gan say,
"Madame, it es oft wemens will
Tham forto blame that sais tham scill."
Sho went oway, als sho noght roght,
And than the lady hyr bythoght,
That the maiden said no wrang,
And so sho sat in stody lang.
In stody thus allane sho sat;
The mayden come ogayn with that.
"Madame," sho said, "ye er a barn;
Thus may ye sone yowre self forfarn."
Sho sayd, "Chastise thi hert, madame;
To swilk a lady it es grete shame
Thus to wepe and make slike cry;
Think opon thi grete gentri.
Trowes thou the flowre of chevalry
Sold al with thi lord dy
And with him be put in molde?
God forbede that it so solde!
Als gude als he and better bene."
"Thou lyes," sho sayd, "by hevyn-quene!
Lat se if thoue me tel kan,
Whar es any so doghty man,
Als he was that wedded me."

113

"Yis, and ye kun me na mawgré,
And that ye mak me sekernes,
That ye sal luf me never the les."
Sho said, "Thou may be ful sertayn,
That for na thing that thou mai sayn,
Wil I me wreth on nane manere."
"Madame," sho said, "than sal ye here;
I sal yow tel a preveté,
And na ma sal it wit bot we.
Yf twa knyghtes be in the felde
On twa stedes with spere and shelde
And the tane the tother may sla,
Whether es the better of tha?"
Sho said, "He that has the bataile."
"Ya," said the mayden, "sawnfayle,
The knyght that lifes es mare of maine
Than yowre lord that was slayne.
Yowre lord fled out of the place,
And the tother gan hym chace
Heder into his awyn halde;
Thare may ye wit, he was ful balde."
The lady said, "This es grete scorne,
That thou nevyns him me biforne;
Thou sais nowther soth ne right.
Swith, out of myne eghen syght!"
The mayden said, "So mot I the,
Thus ne hight ye noght me,
That ye sold so me myssay,"
With that sho turned hir oway,
And hastily sho went ogayn
Unto the chameber to Sir Ywayne.

The lady thoght than al the nyght,

How that sho had na knyght
Forto seke hir land thorghout
To kepe Arthurgh and hys rowt.
Than bigan hir forto shame
And hirself fast forto blame.
Unto hirself fast gan sho flyte
And said, "With wrang now I hir wite.
Now hopes sho I wil never mare
Luf hir als I have done are.
I wil hir luf with main and mode;
For that sho said was for my gode."
   On the morn the mayden rase,
And unto chamber sone sho gase.
Thare sho fyndes the faire lady
Hingand hir hevyd ful drerily
In the place whare sho hir left;
And ilka dele sho talde hir eft,
Als sho had said to hir bifore.
Than said the lady, "Me rewes sore,
That I missayd the yisterday.
I wil amend, if that I may.
Of that knyght now wald I here,
What he war and whethen he were.
I wate that I have sayd omys;
Now wil I do als thou me wys.
Tel me baldely, or thou blin,
If he be cumen of gentil kyn."
"Madame," sho said, "I dar warand,
A genteler lord es none lifand;
The hendest man ye sal him fynde,
That ever come of Adams kynde."
"How hat he? Sai me for sertayne."

"Madame," sho said, "Sir Ywayne;
So gentil knight have ye noght sene;
He es the King son Uryene."
Sho held hir paid of that tithyng,
For that his fader was a kyng;
"Do me have him here in my sight
Bitwene this and the thrid night
And are, if that it are myght be.
Me langes sare him forto se;
Bring him, if thou mai, this night."
    "Madame," sho sayd, "that I ne might,
For his wonyng es hethin oway
More than the jorné of a day.
Bot I have a wele rinand page,
Wil stirt thider right in a stage
And bring him by to-morn at nyght."
The lady saide, "Loke yf he myght
To-morn by evyn be here ogayn."
Sho said, "Madame, with al his mayn."
"Bid him hy on alkyn wyse.
He sal be quit wele his servyse;
Avancement sal be hys bone,
If he wil do this erand sone."
"Madame," sho said, "I dar yow hight
To have him here or the thrid nyght.
Towhils, efter yowre kownsayl send
And ask tham wha sal yow defend
Yowre well, yowre land, kastel, and towre
Ogayns the nobil King Arthure.
For thare es nane of tham ilkane,
That dar the batel undertane.
Than sal ye say, "Nedes bus me take

A lorde to do that ye forsake."
Nedes bus yow have sum nobil knyght,
That wil and may defend yowre right;
And sais also, to suffer ded
Ye wil noght do out of thaire rede.
Of that worde sal thai be blyth
And thank yow ful many sithe."
The lady said, "By God of myght,
I sal areson tham this night.
Me think thou dwelles ful lang here;
Send forth swith the messangere."
   Than was the lady blith and glad.
Sho did al als hir mayden bad.
Efter hir cownsail sho sent onane.
And bad thai sold cum sone ilkane.
The maiden redies hyr ful rath.
Bilive sho gert Syr Ywaine bath
And cled him sethin in gude scarlet
Forord wele and with gold fret,
A girdel ful riche for the nanes
Of perry and of preciows stanes.
Sho talde him al how he sold do,
When that he come the lady to.
And thus when he was al redy,
Sho went and talde to hyr lady,
That cumen was hir messagere.
Sho said smertly, "Do lat me here,
Cumes he sone, als have thou wyn?"
"Medame," sho said, "I sal noght blin,
Or that he be byfor yow here."
Than said the lady with light chere,
"Go bring him heder prevely,

That none wit bot thou and I."
Than the maiden went ogayn
Hastily to Sir Ywayn.
"Sir," sho sayd, "als have I wyn,
My lady wate thou ert hereyn.
To cum bifore hir luke thou be balde,
And tak gode tent what I have talde."
By the hand sho toke the knyght
And led him unto chamber right
Byfor hir lady (es noght at layne),
And of that come was sho ful fayne.
Bot yit Sir Ywayne had grete drede,
When he unto chamber yede.
The chamber flore and als the bed
With klothes of gold was al overspred.
Hir thoght he was withowten lac,
Bot no word to him sho spak.
And he for dred oway he drogh.
Than the mayden stode and logh.
Sho sayd, "Mawgré have that knyght
That haves of swilk a lady syght
And can noght shew to hir his nede.
Cum furth, sir; the thar noght drede,
That mi lady wil the smyte;
Sho loves the wele withouten lite.
Pray to hir of hir mercy,
And for thi sake right so sal I,
That sho forgif the in this stede
Of Salados the Rouse ded,
That was hir lord, that thou has slayne."
    On knese him set than Syr Ywaine.
"Madame, I yelde me yow untill

Ever to be at yowre wyll;
Yf that I might, I ne wald noght fle."
Sho said, "Nay, whi sold so be?
To ded yf I gert do the now,
To me it war ful litel prow.
Bot for I find the so bowsum,
That thou wald thus to me cum,
And for thou dose the in my grace,
I forgif the thi trispase.
Syt down," sho said, "and lat me here,
Why thou ert thus debonere."
"Madame," he said, "anis with a luke,
Al my hert with the thou toke.
Sen I first of the had syght,
Have I the lufed with al my might.
To mo than the, mi lady hende,
Sal never more my luf wende.
For thi luf ever I am redy
Lely forto lif or dy."
Sho said, "Dar thou wele undertake
In my land pese forto make
And forto maintene al mi rightes
Ogayns King Arthure and his knyghtes?"
He said, "That dar I undertane
Ogaynes ilka lyfand man."
Swilk kownsail byfore had sho tane.
Sho said, "Sir, than er we at ane."
Hir barons hir ful rathly red
To tak a lord hir forto wed.

   Than hastily sho went to hall;
Thare abade hir barons all
Forto hald thaire parlement

And mari hir by thaire asent.
Sho sayd, "Sirs, with an acorde,
Sen me bus nedely have a lord
My landes forto lede and yeme,
Sais me sone howe ye wil deme."
"Madame," thai said, "how so ye will,
Al we sal assent thartyll."
   Than the lady went ogayne
Unto chameber to Sir Ywaine.
"Sir," sho said, "so God me save,
Other lorde wil I nane have.
If I the left, I did noght right,
A king son and a noble knyght."
Now has the maiden done hir thoght:
Sir Ywayne out of anger broght.
The lady led him unto hall;
Ogains him rase the barons all.
And al thai said ful sekerly:
"This knight sal wed the lady."
And ilkane said thamself bitwene
(So faire a man had thai noght sene),
"For his bewté in hal and bowre
Him semes to be an emperowre.
We wald that thai war trowth-plight
And weded sone this ilk nyght."
The lady set hir on the dese
And cumand al to hald thaire pese,
And bad hir steward sumwhat say,
Or men went fra cowrt oway.
The steward said, "Sirs, understandes,
Were es waxen in thir landes:
The king Arthure es redy dight

To be here byn this fowretenyght.
He and his menye ha thoght
To win this land if thai moght.
Thai wate ful wele that he es ded,
That was lord here in this stede.
None es so wight wapins to welde
Ne that so boldly mai us belde.
And wemen may maintene no stowre -
Thai most nedes have a governowre.
Tharfor mi lady most nede
Be weded hastily for drede;
And to na lord wil sho tak tent,
Bot if it be by yowre assent."

   Than the lordes al on raw
Held tham wele payd of this saw;
Al assented hyr untill
To tak a lord at hyr owyn wyll.
Than said the lady onone right,
"How hald ye yow paid of this knight?
He profers hym on al wyse
To myne honore and my servyse.
And sertes, sirs, the soth to say,
I saw him never or this day;
Bot talde unto me has it bene,
He es the kyng son Uriene.
He es cumen of hegh parage
And wonder doghty of vasselage.
War and wise and ful curtayse,
He yernes me to wife alwayse.
And nere the lese, I wate, he might
Have wele better, and so war right."
With a voice halely thai sayd,

"Madame, ful wele we hald us payd.
Bot hastes fast, al that ye may,
That ye war wedded this ilk day."
And grete prayer gan thai make
On al wise, that sho suld hym take.
Sone unto the kirk thai went
And war wedded in thaire present.
Thare wedded Ywaine in plevyne
The riche lady Alundyne,
The dukes doghter of Landuit;
Els had hyr lande bene destruyt.
Thus thai made the maryage
Omang al the riche barnage.
Thai made ful mekyl mirth that day,
Ful grete festes on gude aray.
Grete mirthes made thai in that stede,
And al forgetyn es now the ded
Of him that was thaire lord fre.
Thai say that this es worth swilk thre,
And that thai lufed him mekil more
Than him that lord was thare byfore.

 The bridal sat, for soth to tell,
Til Kyng Arthure come to the well
With al his knyghtes everilkane;
Byhind leved thare noght ane.
Than sayd Sir Kay, "Now, whare es he
That made slike bost here forto be
Forto venge his cosyn germayne?
I wist his wordes war al in vayne.
He made grete boste bifor the quene,
And here now dar he noght be sene.
His prowd wordes er now al purst,

For, in fayth, ful ill he durst
Anes luke opon that knyght
That he made bost with to fyght."
Than sayd Gawayn hastily:
"Syr, for Goddes luf, mercy!
For I dar hete the for sertayne,
That we sal here of Sir Ywayne
This ilk day, that be thou balde,
Bot he be ded or done in halde;
And never in no cumpany
Herd I him speke the velany."
Than sayd Sir Kay, "Lo, at thi will
Fra this time forth I sal be still."

   The king kest water on the stane;
The storme rase ful sone onane
With wikked weders, kene and calde,
Als it was byforehand talde.
The king and his men ilkane
Wend tharwith to have bene slane,
So blew it store with slete and rayn;
And hastily than Syr Ywayne
Dight him graythly in his gere
With nobil shelde and strong spere.
When he was dight in seker wede,
Than he umstrade a nobil stede.
Him thoght that he was als lyght
Als a fowl es to the flyght.
Unto the well fast wendes he,
And sone, when thai myght him se,
Syr Kay (for he wald noght fayle)
Smertly askes the batayl.
And alsone than said the kyng,

"Sir Kay, I grante the thine askyng."
Than Sir Ywayn neghed tham nere
Thaire cowntenance to se and here.
Sir Kay than on his stede gan spring;
"Bere the wele now," sayd the kyng.
Ful glad and blith was Syr Ywayne,
When Sir Kay come him ogayn.
Bot Kay wist noght wha it was;
He findes his fere now or he pas.
Syr Ywaine thinkes now to be wroken
On the grete wordes that Kay has spoken.
   Thai rade togeder with speres kene;
Thare was no reverence tham bitwene.
Sir Ywayn gan Sir Kay bere
Out of his sadel lenkith of his spere;
His helm unto the erth smate;
A fote depe tharein yt bate.
He wald do him na more despite,
Bot down he lighted als tyte.
Syr Kay stede he toke in hy
And presand the king ful curtaysly.
Wonder glad than war thai all
That Kay so fowl a shame gan fall;
And ilkone sayd til other then,
"This es he that scornes al men";
Of his wa war thai wele paid.
Syr Ywain than to the kyng said,
"Sir Kyng, I gif to the this stede,
For he may help the in thi nede;
And to me war it grete trispas
Forto withhald that yowres was."
"What man ertow?" quod the kyng;

"Of the have I ne knawyng,
Bot if thou unarmed were
Or els thi name that I might here."
"Lord," he sayd, "I am Ywayne."
Than was the king ferly fayne;
A sari man than was Sir Kay,
That said that he was stollen oway;
Al descumfite he lay on grownde,
To him that was a sary stownde.
The king and his men war ful glad,
That they so Sir Ywayne had,
And ful glad was Sir Gawayne
Of the welefare of Sir Ywayne.
For nane was to him half so dere
Of al that in the court were.
The king Sir Ywayn sone bisoght
To tel him al how he had wroght;
And sone Sir Ywaine gan him tell
Of al his fare how it byfell:
With the knight how that he sped,
And how he had the lady wed,
And how the mayden hym helped wele.
Thus tald he to him ilka dele.
　"Sir King," he sayd, "I yow byseke
And al yowre menye milde and meke,
That ye wald grante to me that grace
At wend with me to my purchace,
And se my kastel and my towre;
Than myght ye do me grete honowre."
The kyng granted him ful right
To dwel with him a fowretenyght.
Sir Ywayne thanked him oft sith;

The knyghtes war al glad and blyth
With Sir Ywaine forto wend.
And sone a squier has he send;
Unto the kastel the way he nome
And warned the lady of thaire come,
And that his lord come with the kyng.
And when the lady herd this thing,
It es no lifand man with mowth,
That half hir cumforth tel kowth.
Hastily that lady hende
Cumand al hir men to wende
And dight tham in thaire best aray
To kepe the king that ilk day.
Thai keped him in riche wede
Rydeand on many a nobil stede;
Thai hailsed him ful curtaysly
And also al his cumpany.
Thai said he was worthy to dowt,
That so fele folk led obowt.
Thare was grete joy, I yow bihete,
With clothes spred in ilka strete
And damysels danceand ful wele
With trompes, pipes, and with fristele.
The castel and the ceté rang
With mynstralsi and nobil sang.
Thai ordand tham ilkane infere
To kepe the king on faire manere.
The lady went withowten towne
And with hir many bald barowne
Cled in purpure and ermyne
With girdels al of gold ful fyne,
The lady made ful meri chere;

Sho was al dight with drewries dere.
Abowt hir was ful mekyl thrang;
The puple cried and sayd omang,
"Welkum ertou, Kyng Arthoure -
Of al this werld thou beres the flowre.
Lord Kyng of all kynges,
And blissed be he that the brynges."
   When the lady the kyng saw,
Unto him fast gan sho draw
To hald his sterap whils he lyght.
Bot sone, when he of hir had syght,
With mekyl myrth thai samen met.
With hende wordes sho him gret,
"A thowsand sithes welkum," sho says,
"And so es Sir Gawayne the curtayse."
The king said, "Lady white so flowre,
God gif the joy and mekil honowre,
For thou ert fayre with body gent."
With that he hir in armes hent,
And ful faire he gan hir falde.
Thare was many to bihalde.
It es no man with tong may tell
The mirth that was tham omell.
Of maidens was thare so gude wane,
That ilka knight myght tak ane.
Ful mekil joy Syr Ywayn made
That he the king til his hows hade;
The lady omang tham al samen
Made ful mekyl joy and gamen.
In the kastel thus thai dwell,
Ful mekyl myrth wase tham omell;
The king was thare with his knyghtes

Aght dayes and aght nyghtes;
And Ywayn tham ful mery made
With alkyn gamyn tham forto glade.
He prayed the kyng to thank the may,
That hym had helpid in his jornay;
And ilk day had thai solace sere
Of huntyng and als of revere;
For thare was a ful fayre cuntré
With wodes and parkes grete plenté,
And castels wroght with lyme and stane,
That Ywayne with his wife had tane.
   Now wil the king no langer lende,
Bot til his cuntré wil he wende.
Aywhils thai war thare, for sertayne,
Syr Gawayn did al his mayne
To pray Sir Ywaine on al manere
Forto wende with tham infere.
He said, "Sir, if thou ly at hame,
Wonderly men wil the blame.
That knight es no thing to set by
That leves al his chevalry
And ligges bekeand in his bed,
When he haves a lady wed.
For when that he has grete endose,
Than war tyme to win his lose;
For when a knyght es chevalrouse,
His lady es the more jelows.
Also sho lufes him wele the bet.
Tharfore, sir, thou sal noght let
To haunt armes in ilk cuntré;
Than wil men wele more prayse the.
Thou hase inogh to thi despens;

Now may thow wele hante turnamentes.
Thou and I sal wende infere,
And I will be at thi banere.
I dar noght say, so God me glad,
If I so fayre a leman had,
That I ne most leve al chevalry
At hame ydel with hir to ly.
Bot yit a fole that litel kan,
May wele cownsail another man."

   So lang Sir Gawayn prayed so,
Syr Ywayne grantes him forto go
Unto the lady and tak his leve;
Loth him was hir forto greve.
Til hyr onane the way he nome,
Bot sho ne wist noght whi he come.
In his arms he gan hir mete,
And thus he said, "My leman swete,
My life, my hele, and al my hert,
My joy, my comforth, and my quert,
A thing prai I the unto
For thine honore and myne also."
The lady said, "Sir, verrayment,
I wil do al yowre cumandment."
"Dame," he said, "I wil the pray,
That I might the king cumvay
And also with my feres founde
Armes forto haunte a stownde.
For in bourding men wald me blame,
If I sold now dwel at hame."

   The lady was loth him to greve.
"Sir," sho said, "I gif yow leve
Until a terme that I sal sayn,

Bot that ye cum than ogayn!
Al this yere hale I yow grante
Dedes of armes forto hante;
Bot, syr, als ye luf me dere,
On al wise that ye be here
This day twelmoth how som it be,
For the luf ye aw to me.
And if ye com noght by that day,
My luf sal ye lose for ay.
Avise yow wele now or ye gone.
This day es the evyn of Saint Jon;
That warn I yow now or ye wende,
Luke ye cum by the twelmoth ende."
"Dame," he sayd, "I sal noght let
To hald the day that thou has set;
And if I might be at my wyll,
Ful oft are sold I cum the till.
Bot, madame, this understandes:
A man that passes divers landes,
May sum tyme cum in grete destres,
In preson or els in sekenes;
Tharfore I pray yow, or I ga,
That ye wil out-tak thir twa."
The lady sayd, "This grant I wele,
Als ye ask, everilka dele;
And I sal lene to yow my ring,
That es to me a ful dere thing.
In nane anger sal ye be,
Whils ye it have and thinkes on me.
I sal tel to yow onane
The vertu that es in the stane:
It es na preson thow sal halde,

Al if yowre fase be manyfalde;
With sekenes sal ye noght be tane,
Ne of yowre blode ye sal lese nane;
In batel tane sal ye noght be,
Whils ye it have and thinkes on me;
And ay, whils ye er trew of love,
Over al sal ye be obove.
I wald never for nakyn wight
Lene it are unto na knyght.
For grete luf I it yow take;
Yemes it wele now for my sake."
Sir Ywayne said, "Dame, gramercy!"
Than he gert ordain in hy
Armurs and al other gere,
Stalworth stedes, both sheld and spere,
And also squyere, knave, and swayne.
Ful glad and blith was Sir Gawayne.
  No lenger wald Syr Ywayne byde,
On his stede sone gan he stride
And thus he has his leve tane.
For him murned many ane.
The lady took leve of the kyng
And of his menye, ald and ying;
Hir lord, Sir Ywayne, sho bisekes
With teris trikland on hir chekes,
On al wise that he noght let
To halde the day that he had set.
The knightes thus thaire ways er went
To justing and to turnament.
Ful dughtily did Sir Ywayne,
And also did Sir Gawayne;
Thai war ful doghty both infere,

Thai wan the prise both fer and nere.
The kyng that time at Cester lay;
The knightes went tham forto play.
Ful really thai rade obout
Al that twelmoth out and out
To justing and to turnament;
Thai wan grete wirships, als thai went;
Sir Ywayne oft had al the lose,
Of him the word ful wide gose;
Of thaire dedes was grete renown
To and fra in towre and towne.
On this wise in this life they last,
Unto Saint Johns day was past.
Then hastily they hied home
And sone unto the kyng thai come;
And thare thai held grete mangeri,
The kyng with al his cumpany.
  Sir Ywaine umbithoght him than,
He had forgeten his leman.
"Broken I have hir cumandment.
Sertes," he said, "now be I shent;
The terme es past that sho me set.
How ever sal this bale be bet?
Unnethes he might him hald fra wepe.
And right in this than toke he kepe,
Into court come a damysele
On a palfray ambland wele;
And egerly down gan sho lyght
Withouten help of knave or knyght.
And sone sho lete hyr mantel fall
And hasted hir fast into hall.
"Syr Kyng," sho sayde, "God mot the se,

My lady gretes the wele by me,
And also Sir gude Gawayne
And al thi knyghtes bot Sir Ywayne.
He es ateyned for trayture,
A fals and lither losenjoure;
He has bytrayed my lady,
But sho es war with his gilry.
Sho hopid noght, the soth to say,
That he wald so have stollen oway.
He made to hir ful mekyl boste
And said, of al he lufed hir moste.
Al was treson and trechery,
And that he sal ful dere haby.
It es ful mekyl ogains the right
To cal so fals a man a knight.
My lady wend he had hir hert
Ay forto kepe and hald in quert,
Bot now with grefe he has hir gret
And broken the term that sho him set,
That was the evyn of Saynt John;
Now es that tyme for ever gone.
So lang gaf sho him respite,
And thus he haves hir led with lite.
Sertainly, so fals a fode
Was never cumen of kynges blode,
That so sone forgat his wyfe,
That lofed him better than hyr life."
Til Ywayne sais sho thus, "Thou es
Traytur untrew and trowthles
And also an unkind cumlyng.
Deliver me my lady ring!
Sho stirt to him with sterne loke,

The ring fro his finger sho toke;
And alsone als sho had the ring,
Hir leve toke sho of the king
And stirted up on hir palfray.
Withowten more sho went hir way;
With hir was nowther knave ne grome,
Ne no man wist where sho bycome.
    Sir Ywayn, when he this gan here,
Murned and made simpil chere;
In sorrow than so was he stad,
That nere for murning wex he mad.
It was no mirth that him myght mend;
At worth to noght ful wele he wend,
For wa he es ful wil of wane.
"Allas, I am myne owin bane;
Allas," he sayd, "that I was born,
Have I my leman thus forlorn,
And al es for myne owen foly.
Allas, this dole wil mak me dy."
An evyl toke him als he stode;
For wa he wex al wilde and wode.
Unto the wod the way he nome;
No man wist whore he bycome.
Obout he welk in the forest,
Als it wore a wilde beste;
His men on ilka syde has soght
Fer and nere and findes him noght.
    On a day als Ywayne ran
In the wod, he met a man;
Arowes brade and bow had he,
And when Sir Ywayne gan him se,
To him he stirt with bir ful grim,

His bow and arwes reft he him.
Ilka day than at the leste
Shot he him a wilde beste;
Fless he wan him ful gude wane,
And of his arows lost he nane.
Thare he lifed a grete sesowne;
With rotes amd raw venysowne;
He drank of the warm blode,
And that did him mekil gode.

   Als he went in that boskage,
He fand a litil ermytage.
The ermyte saw and sone was war,
A naked man a bow bare.
He hoped he was wode that tide;
Tharfore no lenger durst he bide.
He sperd his gate and in he ran
Forfered of that wode man;
And for him thoght it charité,
Out at his window set he
Brede and water for the wode man;
And tharto ful sone he ran.
Swilk als he had, swilk he him gaf,
Barly-brede with al the chaf;
Tharof ete he ful gude wane,
And are swilk ete he never nane.
Of the water he drank tharwith;
Than ran he forth into the frith,
For if a man be never so wode,
He wil kum whare man dose him gode,
And, sertanly, so did Ywayne.
Everilka day he come ogayne,
And with him broght he redy boun

135

Ilka day new venisowne;
He laid it at the ermite gate
And ete and drank and went his gate.
Ever alsone als he was gane,
The ermyt toke the flesh onane;
He flogh it and seth it fayre and wele;
Than had Ywayne at ilka mele
Brede and sothen venysowne.
Than went the ermyte to the towne
And salde the skinnes that he broght,
And better brede tharwith he boght;
Than fand Sir Ywayne in that stede
Venyson and better brede.
This life led he ful fele yere,
And sethen he wroght als ye sal here.
   Als Ywaine sleped under a tre,
By him come thare rideand thre:
A lady, twa bourewemen alswa.
Than spak ane of the maidens twa,
"A naked man me think I se;
Wit I wil what it may be."
Sho lighted doun and to him yede,
And unto him sho toke gude hede;
Hir thoght wele sho had him sene
In many stedes whare sho had bene.
Sho was astonyd in that stownde,
For in hys face sho saw a wonde,
Bot it was heled and hale of hew;
Tharby, hir thoght, that sho him knew.
Sho sayd, "By God that me has made,
Swilk a wound Sir Ywayne hade.
Sertaynly, this ilk es he.

Allas," sho sayd, "how may this be?
Allas, that him es thus bityd,
So nobil a knyght als he was kyd.
It es grete sorow that he sold be
So ugly now opon to se."
So tenderly for him sho gret,
That hir teres al hir chekes wet.
"Madame," sho said, "for sertayn,
Here have we funden Sir Ywayne,
The best knyght that on grund mai ga.
Allas, him es bytid so wa;
In sum sorow was he stad,
And tharfore es he waxen mad.
Sorow wil meng a mans blode
And make him forto wax wode.
Madame, and he war now in quert
And al hale of will and hert,
Ogayns yowre fa he wald yow were,
That has yow done so mekyl dere.
And he ware hale, so God me mend,
Yowre sorow war sone broght to end."
The lady said, "And this ilk be he
And than he wil noght hethin fle,
Thorgh Goddes help than, hope I yit
We sal him win ynto his wyt.
Swith at hame I wald we were,
For thare I have an unement dere;
Morgan the Wise gaf it to me
And said als I sal tel to the.
He sayd, "This unement es so gode,
That if a man be braynwode
And he war anes anoynt with yt,

137

Smertly sold he have his wit."
  Fro hame thai wer bot half a myle;
Theder come thai in a whyle.
The lady sone the boyst has soght,
And the unement has sho broght.
"Have," sho said, "this unement here,
Unto me it es ful dere;
And smertly that thou wend ogayne.
Bot luke thou spend it noght in vaine;
And fra the knight anoynted be,
That thou leves, bring it to me."
Hastily that maiden meke
Tok hose and shose and serk and breke.
A riche robe als gan sho ta
And a saint of silk alswa
And also a gude palfray,
And smertly come sho whare he lay.
On slepe fast yit sho him fande.
Hir hors until a tre sho band,
And hastily to him sho yede,
And that was ful hardy dede.
Sho enoynt hys heved wele
And his body ilka dele.
Sho despended al the unement
Over hir ladies cumandment.
For hir lady wald sho noght let;
Hir thoght that it was ful wele set.
Al his atyre sho left hym by
At his rising to be redy
That he might him cleth and dyght,
Or he sold of hyr have syght.
  Than he wakend of his slepe;

The maiden to him toke gude kepe;
He luked up ful sarily
And said, "Lady Saynt Mary,
What hard grace to me es maked,
That I am here now thus naked?
Allas, wher any have here bene?
I trow, sum has my sorow sene."
Lang he sat so in a thoght,
How that gere was theder broght.
Than had he noght so mekyl myght
On his fote to stand upright;
Him failed might of fote and hand,
That he myght nowther ga ne stand.
Bot yit his clathes on he wan;
Tharfore ful wery was he than.
Than had he mister forto mete
Sum man that myght his bales bete.
Than lepe the maiden on hir palfray
And nere byside him made hir way.
Sho lete als sho him noght had sene
Ne wetyn that he thare had bene.
Sone when he of hir had syght,
He cried unto hyr on hight.
Than wald sho no ferrer ride,
Bot fast sho luked on ilka syde
And waited obout fer and nere.
He cried and sayd, "I am here."
Than sone sho rade him till
And sayd, "Sir, what es thi will?"
"Lady, thi help war me ful lefe,
For I am here in grete meschefe.
I ne wate never by what chance

That I have al this grevance.
Thar charité I walde the pray
Forto lene me that palfray,
That in thi hand es redy bowne
And wis me sone unto som towne.
I wate noght how I had this wa,
Ne how that I sal hethin ga."
Sho answered him with wordes hende,
"Syr, if thou wil with me wende,
Ful gladly wil I ese the,
Until that thou amended be."
   Sho helped him up on his hors ryg,
And sone thai come until a bryg;
Into the water the boist sho cast,
And sethin hame sho hied fast.
When thai come to the castel gate,
Thai lighted and went in tharate.
The maiden to the chameber went;
The lady asked the unement.
"Madame," sho said, "the boyst es lorn,
And so was I nerehand tharforn."
"How so," sho said, "for Goddes Tre?"
"Madame," she said, "I sal tel the
Al the soth how that it was.
Als I over the brig sold pas,
Evyn in myddes, the soth to say,
Thare stombild my palfray;
On the brig he fell al flat,
And the boyst right with that
Fel fra me in the water down;
And had I noght bene titter boun
To tak my palfray by the mane,

The water sone had bene my bane."
The lady said, "Now am I shent,
That I have lorn my gude unement;
It was to me, so God me glade,
The best tresure that ever I hade.
To me it es ful mekil skath,
Bot better es lose it than yow bath.
"Wend," sho said, "unto the knight
And luke thou ese him at thi myght."
"Lady," sho said, "els war me lathe."
Than sho gert him washe and bathe
And gaf him mete and drink of main,
Til he had geten his might ogayn.
Thai ordand armurs ful wele dight,
And so thai did stedes ful wight.

   So it fell sone on a day,
Whils he in the castel lay,
The ryche eryl, Syr Alers,
With knightes, serjantes and swiers,
And with swith grete vetale
Come that kastel to asayle.
Sir Ywain than his armurs tase
With other socure that he hase.
The erel he kepes in the felde,
And sone he hit ane on the shelde,
That the knyght and als the stede
Stark ded to the erth thai yede.
Sone another, the thrid, the ferth
Feld he doun ded on the erth;
He stird him so omang tham than,
At ilka dint he slogh a man.
Sum he losed of hys men,

Bot the eril lost swilk ten.
Al thai fled fast fra that syde,
Whare thai saw Sir Ywayn ride.
He herted so his cumpany,
The moste coward was ful hardy
To fel al that thai fand in felde.
　　The lady lay ever and bihelde;
Sho sais, "Yon es a nobil knyght,
Ful eger and of ful grete myght;
He es wele worthy forto prayse,
That es so doghty and curtayse."
The mayden said, "Withowten let,
Yowre oynement may ye think wele set;
Sese, madame, how he prikes,
And sese also how fele he stikes
Lo, how he fars omang his fase;
Al that he hittes sone he slase.
War thare swilk other twa als he,
Than, hope I, sone thaire fase sold fle.
Sertes, than sold we se ful tyte,
The eril sold be descumfite.
Madame, God gif, his wil were
To wed yow and be loverd here."
The erils folk went fast to ded;
To fle than was his best rede.
The eril sone bigan to fle,
And than might men bourd se,
How Sir Ywayne and his feres
Folowd tham on fel maners;
And fast thai slogh the erils men,
Olive thai left noght over ten.
The eril fled ful fast for drede,

And than Sir Ywaine strake his stede
And overtoke him in that tide
At a kastel thar bysyde.
Sir Ywayne sone withset the gate,
That the eril myght noght in tharate.
The eril saw al might noght gain;
He yalde him sone to Sir Ywayn.
And sone he has his trowth plyght
To wend with him that ilk night
Unto the lady of grete renowne
And profer him to hir presowne,
And to do him in hir grace
And also to mend his trispase.
  The eril than unarmed his hevid,
And none armure on him he levid.
Helm, shelde, and als his brand,
That he bare naked in his hand,
Al he gaf to Sir Ywayne,
And hame with him he went ogaine.
In the kastel made thai joy ilkane,
When thai wist the eril was tane.
And, when thai saw tham cumand nere,
Ogayns him went thai al infere;
And when the lady gan tham mete,
Sir Ywaine gudely gan hir grete.
He said, "Madame, have thi presoun
And hald him here in thi baundoun."
Bot he gert hir grante him grace
To mak amendes yn that space.
On a buke the erl sware
Forto restore bath les and mare,
And big ogayn bath toure and toune,

That by him war casten doune,
And evermare to be hir frende.
Umage made he to that hende;
To this forward he borows fand,
The best lordes of al that land.
　　Sir Ywaine wald no lenger lend,
Bot redies him fast forto wend.
At the lady his leve he takes,
Grete murnyng tharfore sho makes.
Sho said, "Sir, if it be yowre will,
I pray yow forto dwel here still;
And I wil yelde into yowre handes
Myne awyn body and al my landes."
Hereof fast sho hym bysoght,
Bot al hir speche avayles noght.
He said, "I wil no thing to mede
Bot myne armurs and my stede."
Sho said, "Bath stede and other thing
Es yowres at yowre owyn likyng;
And if ye walde here with us dwell,
Mekyl mirth war us omell."
It was na bote to bid him bide,
He toke his stede and on gan stride;
The lady and hyr maydens gent
Wepid sare when that he went.
　　Now rides Ywayn als ye sal here,
With hevy herte and dreri chere
Thurgh a forest by a sty;
And thare he herd a hydose cry.
The gaynest way ful sone he tase,
Til he come whare the noys was.
Than was he war of a dragoun,

144

Had asayled a wilde lyown;
With his tayl he drogh him fast,
And fire ever on him he cast.
The lyoun had over litel myght
Ogaynes the dragon forto fyght.
Than Sir Ywayn made him bown
Forto sucore the lyown;
His shelde bifore his face he fest
For the fyre that the dragon kest;
He strake the dragon in at the chavyl,
That it come out at the navyl.
Sunder strake he the throte-boll,
That fra the body went the choll.
By the lioun tail the hevid hang yit,
For tharby had he tane his bit;
The tail Sir Ywayne strake in twa,
The dragon hevid than fel tharfra.
He thoght, "If the lyoun me asayle,
Redy sal he have batayle."
Bot the lyoun wald noght fyght.
Grete fawnyng made he to the knyght.
Down on the grund he set him oft,
His fortherfete he held oloft,
And thanked the knyght als he kowth,
Al if he myght noght speke with mowth;
So wele the lyon of him lete,
Ful law he lay and likked his fete.
When Syr Ywayne that sight gan se,
Of the beste him thoght peté,
And on his wai forth gan he ride;
The lyown folowd by hys syde.
In the forest al that day

The lyoun mekely foloud ay,
And never for wele ne for wa
Wald he part Sir Ywayn fra.
    Thus in the forest als thai ware,
The lyoun hungerd swith sare.
Of a beste savore he hade;
Until hys lord sembland he made,
That he wald go to get his pray;
His kind it wald, the soth to say.
For his lorde sold him noght greve,
He wald noght go withowten leve.
Fra his lord the way he laght
The mountance of ane arow-draght;
Sone he met a barayn da,
And ful sone he gan hir sla;
Hir throte in twa ful sone he bate
And drank the blode whils it was hate.
That da he kest than in his nek,
Als it war a mele sek.
Unto his lorde than he it bare;
And Sir Ywayn parsayved thare,
That it was so nere the nyght,
That no ferrer ride he might.
    A loge of bowes sone he made,
And flynt and fire-yren bath he hade,
And fire ful sone thare he slogh
Of dry mos and many a bogh.
The lion has the da undone;
Sire Ywayne made a spit ful sone,
And rosted sum to thaire sopere.
The lyon lay als ye sal here:
Unto na mete he him drogh

Until his maister had eten ynogh.
Him failed thare bath salt and brede,
And so him did whyte wine and rede;
Bot of swilk thing als thai had,
He and his lyon made tham glad.
The lyon hungerd for the nanes,
Ful fast he ete raw fless and banes.
Sir Ywayn in that ilk telde
Laid his hevid opon his shelde;
Al nyght the lyon about gede
To kepe his mayster and his stede.
Thus the lyon and the knyght
Lended thare a fouretenyght.

   On a day so it byfell,
Syr Ywayne come unto the well.
He saw the chapel and the thorne
And said allas that he was born;
And when he loked on the stane,
He fel in swowing sone onane.
Als he fel his swerde outshoke;
The pomel into the erth toke,
The poynt toke until his throte -
Wel nere he made a sari note!
Thorgh his armurs sone it smate,
A litel intil hys hals it bate;
And wen the lyon saw his blude,
He brayded als he had bene wode.
Than kest he up so lathly rerde,
Ful mani fok myght he have ferde.
He wend wele, so God me rede,
That his mayster had bene ded.
It was ful grete peté to here

What sorow he made on his manere.
He stirt ful hertly, I yow hete,
And toke the swerde bytwix his fete;
Up he set it by a stane,
And thare he wald himself have slane;
And so he had sone, for sertayne,
Bot right in that rase Syr Ywayne;
And alsone als he saw hym stand,
For fayn he liked fote and hand.
Sir Ywayn said oft sithes, "Allas,
Of alkins men hard es my grace.
Mi leman set me sertayn day,
And I it brak, so wayloway.
Allas, for dole how may I dwell
To se this chapel and this well,
Hir faire thorn, hir riche stane?
My gude dayes er now al gane,
My joy es done now al bidene,
I am noght worthi to be sene.
I saw this wild beste was ful bayn
For my luf himself have slayne.
Than sold I, sertes, by more right
Sla my self for swilk a wyght
That I have for my foly lorn.
Allas the while that I was born!"
    Als Sir Ywayn made his mane
In the chapel ay was ane
And herd his murnyng haly all
Thorgh a crevice of the wall,
And sone it said with simepel chere,
"What ertou, that murnes here?"
"A man," he sayd, "sum tyme I was.

What ertow? Tel me or I pas."
"I am," it sayd, "the sariest wight,
That ever lifed by day or nyght."
"Nay," he said, "by Saynt Martyne,
Thare es na sorow mete to myne,
Ne no wight so wil of wane.
I was a man, now am I nane;
Whilom I was a nobil knyght
And a man of mekyl myght;
I had knyghtes of my menye
And of reches grete plenté;
I had a ful fayre seignory,
And al I lost for my foly.
Mi maste sorow als sal thou here:
I lost a lady that was me dere."
The tother sayd, "Allas, allas,
Myne es a wele sarier case:
To-morn I mun bere my jewyse,
Als my famen wil devise."
"Allas," he said, "what es the skill?"
"That sal thou here, sir, if thou will.
I was a mayden mekil of pride
With a lady here nere biside;
Men me bikalles of tresown
And has me put here in presown.
I have no man to defend me,
Tharfore to-morn brent mun I be."
He sayd, "What if thou get a knyght,
That for the with thi fase wil fight?"
"Sir," sho sayd, "als mot I ga,
In this land er bot knyghtes twa,
That me wald help to cover of care:

149

The tane es went, I wate noght whare;
The tother es dweland with the king
And wate noght of my myslykyng.
The tane of tham hat Syr Gawayn.
And the tother hat Syr Ywayn.
For hym sal I be done to dede
To-morn right in this same stede;
He es the Kinges son Uriene."
"Parfay," he sayd, "I have hym sene;
I am he, and for my gilt
Sal thou never more be spilt.
Thou ert Lunet, if I can rede,
That helpyd me yn mekyl drede;
I had bene ded had thou noght bene.
Tharfore tel me us bytwene,
How bical thai the of treson
Thus forto sla and for what reson?"
"Sir, thai say that my lady
Lufed me moste specially,
And wroght al efter my rede;
Tharefore thai hate me to the ded.
The steward says that done have I
Grete tresone unto my lady.
His twa brether sayd it als,
And I wist that thai said fals;
And sone I answerd als a sot -
For fole bolt es sone shot -
I said that I sold find a knyght,
That sold me mayntene in my right
And feght with tham al thre;
Thus the batayl wajed we.
Than thai granted me als tyte

Fourty dayes unto respite;
And at the kynges court I was;
I fand na cumfort ne na solase
Nowther of knyght, knave, ne swayn."
Than said he, "Whare was Syr Gawayn?
He has bene ever trew and lele,
He fayled never no damysele."
Scho said, "In court he was noght sene,
For a knyght led oway the quene.
The king tharfore es swith grym;
Syr Gawayn folowd efter him,
He coms noght hame, for sertayne,
Until he bryng the quene ogayne.
Now has thou herd, so God me rede,
Why I sal be done to ded."
He said, "Als I am trew knyght,
I sal be redy forto fyght
To-morn with tham al thre,
Leman, for the luf of the.
At my might I sal noght fayl.
Bot how so bese of the batayle,
If ani man my name the frayne,
On al manere luke thou yt layne;
Unto na man my name thou say."
"Syr," sho sayd, "for soth, nay.
I prai to grete God alweldand,
That thai have noght the hegher hand;
Sen that ye wil my murnyng mend,
I tak the grace that God wil send."
Syr Ywayn sayd, "I sal the hyght
To mend thi murnyng at my myght:
Thorgh grace of God in Trenyté

I sal the wreke of tham al thre."
   Than rade he forth into frith,
And hys lyoun went hym with.
Had he redyn bot a stownde,
A ful fayre castell he fownde;
And Syr Ywaine, the soth to say,
Unto the castel toke the way.
When he come at the castel gate,
Foure porters he fand tharate.
The drawbryg sone lete thai doun,
Bot al thai fled for the lyown.
Thai said, "Syr, withowten dowt,
That beste byhoves the leve tharout."
He sayd, "Sirs, so have I wyn,
Mi lyoun and I sal noght twyn;
I luf him als wele, I yow hete,
Als my self at ane mete;
Owther sal we samyn lende,
Or els wil we hethin wende.
Bot right with that the lord he met,
And ful gladly he him gret,
With knyghtes and swiers grete plenté
And faire ladies and maydens fre;
Ful mekyl joy of him thai made,
Bot sorow in thaire hertes thai hade.
Unto a chameber was he led
And unharmed and sethin cled
In clothes that war gay and dere.
Bot ofttymes changed thaire chere;
Sum tyme, he saw, thai weped all
Als ai wald to water fall;
Thai made slike murnyng and slik mane

That gretter saw he never nane;
Thai feynyd tham oft for hys sake
Fayre semblant forto make.
Ful grete wonder Sir Ywayn hade
For thai swilk joy and sorow made.
"Sir," he said, "if yowre wil ware,
I wald wyt why ye make slike kare."
"This joy," he said, "that we mak now,
Sir, es al for we have yow;
And, sir, also we mak this sorow
For dedys that sal be done to-morow.
A geant wons here nere bysyde,
That es a devil of mekil pryde;
His name hat Harpyns of Mowntain.
For him we lyf in mekil payn;
My landes haves he robbed and reft,
Noght bot this kastel es me left.
And, by God that in hevyn wons,
Syr, I had sex knyghtis to sons;
I saw my self the twa slogh he,
To-morn the foure als slane mun be -
He has al in hys presowne.
And, sir, for nane other enchesowne,
Bot for I warned hym to wyve
My doghter, fayrest fode olyve.
Tharfore es he wonder wrath,
And depely has he sworn hys ath,
With maystry that he sal hir wyn,
And that the laddes of his kychyn
And also that his werst fote-knave
His wil of that woman sal have,
Bot I to-morn might find a knight,

That durst with hym selven fyght;
And I have none to him at ga.
What wonder es if me be wa?"
　　Syr Ywayn lystend hym ful wele,
And when he had talde ilka dele,
"Syr," he sayd, "me think mervayl
That ye soght never no kounsayl
At the kynges hous here bysyde;
For, sertes, in al this werld so wyde
Es no man of so mekil myght,
Geant, champioun, ne knight,
That he ne has knyghtes of his menye
That ful glad and blyth wald be
Forto mete with swilk a man
That thai myght kyth thaire myghtes on."
He said, "Syr, so God me mend,
Unto the kynges kourt I send
To seke my mayster Syr Gawayn;
For he wald socore me ful fain.
He wald noght leve for luf ne drede,
Had he wist now of my nede;
For his sister es my wyfe,
And he lufes hyr als his lyfe.
Bot a knyght this other day,
Thai talde, has led the quene oway.
Forto seke hyr went Sir Gawayn,
And yit ne come he noght ogayn."
Than Syr Ywayne sighed sare
And said unto the knyght right thare;
"Syr," he sayd, "for Gawayn sake
This batayl wil I undertake
Forto fyght with the geant;

And that opon swilk a covenant,
Yif he cum at swilk a time,
So that we may fight by prime.
No langer may I tent tharto,
For other thing I have to do;
I have a dede that most be done
To-morn nedes byfor the none."
The knyght sare sighand sayd him till,
"Sir, God yelde the thi gode wyll."
And al that ware thare in the hall,
On knese byfor hym gan thai fall.
Forth thare come a byrd ful bryght,
The fairest man might se in sight;
Hir moder come with hir infere,
And both thai morned and made yll chere.
The knight said, "Lo, verraiment,
God has us gude socure sent,
This knight that of his grace wil grant
Forto fyght with the geant."
On knese thai fel doun to his fete
And thanked him with wordes swete.
"A, God forbede," said Sir Ywain,
"That the sister of Sir Gawayn
Or any other of his blode born
Sold on this wise knel me byforn."
He toke tham up tyte both infere
And prayd tham to amend thaire chere.
"And praies fast to God alswa,
That I may venge yow on yowre fa,
And that he cum swilk tyme of day,
That I by tyme may wend my way
Forto do another dede;

For, sertes, theder most I nede.
Sertes, I wald noght tham byswike
Forto win this kinges rike."
His thoght was on that damysel,
That he left in the chapel.
Thai said, "He es of grete renowne,
For with hym dwels the lyoun."
Ful wele confort war thai all
Bath in boure and als in hall.
Ful glad war thai of thaire gest,
And when tyme was at go to rest,
The lady broght him to his bed;
And for the lyoun sho was adred.
Na man durst negh his chamber nere,
Fro thai war broght thareyn infere.
Sone at morn, when it was day,
The lady and the fayre may
Til Ywayn chamber went thai sone,
And the dore thai have undone.
  Sir Ywayn to the kyrk gede
Or he did any other dede;
He herd the servise of the day
And sethin to the knyght gan say,
"Sir," he said, "now most I wend,
Lenger here dar I noght lende;
Til other place byhoves me fare."
Than had the knyght ful mekel care;
He said, "Syr, dwells a litel thraw
For luf of Gawayn that ye knaw;
Socore us now or ye wende.
I sal yow gif withowten ende
Half my land with toun and toure,

And ye wil help us in this stoure."
Sir Ywayn said, "Nai, God forbede
That I sold tak any mede."
Than was grete dole, so God me glade,
To se the sorow that thai made.
Of tham Sir Ywayn had grete peté;
Him thoght his hert myght breke in thre,
For in grete drede ay gan he dwell
For the mayden in the chapell.
For, sertes, if sho war done to ded,
Of him war than none other rede
Bot oither he sold hymselven sla
Or wode ogain to the wod ga.
  Ryght with that thare come a grome
And said tham that geant come:
"Yowre sons bringes he him byforn,
Wel nere naked als thai war born."
With wreched ragges war thai kled
And fast bunden; thus er thai led.
The geant was bath large and lang
And bare a levore of yren ful strang;
Tharwith he bet tham bitterly.
Grete rewth it was to here tham cry;
Thai had no thing tham forto hyde.
A dwergh gode on the tother syde,
He bare a scowrge with cordes ten;
Tharewith he bet tha gentil men
Ever on ane als he war wode.
Efter ilka band brast out the blode;
And when thai at the walles were,
He cried loud that men myght here,
"If thou wil have thi sons in hele,

Deliver me that damysele.
I sal hir gif to warisowne
Ane of the foulest quisteroun,
That ever yit ete any brede.
He sal have hir maydenhede.
Thar sal none other lig hir by
Bot naked herlotes and lowsy."
When the lord thir wordes herd,
Als he war wode for wa he ferd.
Sir Ywayn than that was curtays,
Unto the knyght ful sone he sais:
"This geant es ful fers and fell
And of his wordes ful kruell;
I sal deliver hir of his aw
Or els be ded within a thraw.
For, sertes, it war a misaventure
That so gentil a creature
Sold ever so foul hap byfall
To be defouled with a thrall."
Sone was he armed, Sir Ywayn;
Tharfore the ladies war ful fayn.
Thai helpid to lace him in his wede,
And sone he lepe up on his stede.
Thai prai to God that grace him grant
Forto sla that foul geant.
The drawbrigges war laten doun,
And forth he rides with his lioun.
Ful mani sari murnand man
Left he in the kastel than,
That on thaire knese to God of might
Praied ful hertly for the knyght.
   Syr Ywayn rade into the playne,

And the geant come hym ogayne.
His levore was ful grete and lang
And himself ful mekyl and strang;
He said, "What devil made the so balde
Forto cum heder out of thi halde?
Whosoever the heder send,
Lufed the litel, so God me mend.
Of the he wald be wroken fayn."
"Do forth thi best," said Sir Ywayn.
Al the armure he was yn,
Was noght bot of a bul-skyn.
Sir Ywayn was to him ful prest,
He strake to him in middes the brest.
The spere was both stif and gode -
Whare it toke bit, outbrast the blode.
So fast Sir Ywayn on yt soght,
The bul-scyn availed noght.
The geant stombild with the dynt,
And unto Sir Ywayn he mynt,
And on the shelde he hit ful fast,
It was mervayl that it myght last.
The levore bended tharwithall,
With grete force he lete it fall,
The geant was so strong and wight,
That never for no dint of knyght
Ne for batayl that he sold make,
Wald he none other wapyn take.
Sir Ywain left his spere of hand
And strake obout him with his brand,
And the geant mekil of mayn
Strake ful fast to him ogayn,
Til at the last within a throw

He rest him on his sadelbow;
And that parcayved his lioun,
That his hevid so hanged doun,
He hopid that hys lord was hyrt,
And to the geant sone he styrt.
The scyn and fless bath rafe he down
Fro his hals to hys cropoun;
His ribbes myght men se onane,
For al was bare unto bane.
At the lyown oft he mynt,
Bot ever he lepis fro his dynt,
So that no strake on him lyght.
By than was Ywain cumen to myght,
Than wil he wreke him if he may.
The geant gaf he ful gude pay;
He smate oway al his left cheke,
His sholder als of gan he kleke,
That both his levore and his hand
Fel doun law opon the land.
Sethin with a stoke to him he stert
And smate the geant unto the hert:
Than was nane other tale to tell,
Bot fast unto the erth he fell,
Als it had bene a hevy tre.
Than myght men in the kastel se
Ful mekil mirth on ilka side.
The gates kest thai opyn wyde;
The lord unto Syr Ywaine ran,
Him foloud many a joyful man;
Also the lady ran ful fast,
And hir doghter was noght the last.
I may noght tel the joy thai had;

And the foure brether war ful glad,
For thai war out of bales broght.
The lord wist it helpid noght
At pray Sir Ywayn for to dwell,
For tales that he byfore gan tell.
Bot hertly with his myght and mayn
He praied him forto cum ogayn
And dwel with him a litel stage,
When he had done hys vassage.
He said, "Sir, that may I noght do;
Bileves wele, for me bus go."
Tham was ful wo - he wald noght dwell -
Bot fain thai war that it so fell.

  The neghest way than gan he wele,
Until he come to the chapele.
Thare he fand a mekil fire
And the mayden with lely lire
In hyr smok was bunden fast
Into the fire forto be kast.
Unto himself he sayd in hy
And prayed to God almyghty,
That he sold for his mekil myght
Save fro shame that swete wight.
"Yf thai be many and mekil of pryse,
I sal let for no kouwardise;
For with me es bath God and right,
And thai sal help me forto fight.
And my lyon sal help me -
Than er we foure ogayns tham thre."
Sir Ywayn rides and cries then,
"Habides, I bid yow, fals men!
It semes wele that ye er wode,

That wil spill this sakles blode.
Ye sal noght so, yf that I may."
His lyown made hym redy way.
Naked he saw the mayden stand
Bihind hir bunden aither hand:
Than sighed Ywain wonder-oft,
Unnethes might he syt oloft.
Thare was no sembland tham bitwene,
That ever owther had other sene.
Al obout hyr myght men se
Ful mykel sorow and grete peté
Of other ladies that thare were,
Wepeand with ful sory chere.
"Lord," thai sayd, "what es oure gylt?
Oure joy, oure confort sal be spilt.
Who sal now oure erandes say?
Allas, who sal now for us pray?"
Whils thai thus karped, was Lunet
On knese byfore the prest set,
Of hir syns hir forto schrive.
And unto hir he went bylive,
Hir hand he toke, and up sho rase;
"Leman," he sayd, "whore er thi fase?"
"Sir, lo tham yonder in yone stede
Bideand until I be ded;
Thai have demed me with wrang.
Wel nere had ye dwelt over lang!
I pray to God He do yow mede
That ye wald help me in this nede."
Thir wordes herd than the steward;
He hies him unto hir ful hard.
He said, "Thou lies, fals woman!

For thi treson ertow tane.
Sho has bitraied hir lady,
And, sir, so wil sho the in hy.
And tharfore, syr, by Goddes dome,
I rede thou wend right als thou com;
Thou takes a ful febil rede,
If thou for hir will suffer ded."
Unto the steward than said he,
"Who so es ferd, I rede he fle;
And, sertes, I have bene this day,
Whare I had ful large pay;
And yit," he sayd, "I sal noght fail."
To tham he waged the batayl.
"Do oway thi lioun," said the steward,
"For that es noght oure forward.
Allane sal thou fight with us thre."
And unto him thus answerd he,
"Of my lioun no help I crave;
I ne have none other fote-knave;
If he wil do yow any dere,
I rede wele that ye yow were."
The steward said, "On alkins wise
Thi lyoun, sir, thou most chastise,
That he do here no harm this day,
Or els wend forth on thi way;
For hir warand mai thou noght be,
Bot thou allane fight with us thre.
Al thir men wote, and so wote I,
That sho bitrayed hir lady.
Als traytures sal sho have hyre,
Sho be brent here in this fire."
Sir Ywayn sad, "Nai, God forbede!"

(He wist wele how the soth gede.)
"I trow to wreke hir with the best.'
He bad his lyoun go to rest;
And he laid him sone onane
Doun byfore tham everilkane;
Bitwene his legges he layd his tail
And so biheld to the batayl.
   Al thre thai ride to Sir Ywayn,
And smertly rides he tham ogayn;
In that time nothing tint he,
For his an strake was worth thaires thre.
He strake the steward on the shelde,
That he fel doun flat in the felde;
Bot up he rase yit at the last
And to Sir Ywayn strake ful fast.
Tharat the lyoun greved sare;
No lenger wald he than lig thare.
To help his mayster he went onane;
And the ladies everilkane,
That war thare forto se that sight,
Praied ful fast ay for the knight.
   The lyoun hasted him ful hard,
And sone he come to the steward.
A ful fel mynt to him he made:
He bigan at the shulder-blade,
And with his pawm al rafe he downe
Bath hauberk and his actoune
And al the fless doun til his kne,
So that men myght his guttes se;
To ground he fell so al torent
Was thare no man that him ment.
The lioun gan hym sla.

Than war thai bot twa and twa,
And, sertanly, thare Sir Ywayn
Als with wordes did his main
Forto chastis hys lyowne;
Bot he ne wald na more lig doun.
The liown thoght, how so he sayd,
That with his help he was wele payd.
Thai smate the lyoun on ilka syde
And gaf him many woundes wide.
When that he saw hys lyoun blede,
He ferd for wa als he wald wede,
And fast he strake than in that stoure,
Might thare none his dintes doure.
So grevosly than he bygan
That doun he bare bath hors and man.
Thai yald tham sone to Sir Ywayn,
And tharof war the folk ful fayne;
And sone quit to tham thaire hire,
For both he kest tham in the fire
And said, "Wha juges men with wrang,
The same jugement sal thai fang."
Thus he helpid the maiden ying,
And sethin he made the saghtelyng
Bitwene hyr and the riche lady.
    Than al the folk ful hastily
Proferd tham to his servise
To wirship him ever on al wise.
Nane of tham al wist bot Lunet
That thai with thaire lord war met.
The lady prayed him als the hend
That he hame with tham wald wende
Forto sojorn thare a stownd,

165

Til he wer warist of his wound.
By his sare set he noght a stra,
Bot for his lioun was him wa.
"Madame," he said, "sertes, nay,
I mai noght dwel, the soth to say."
Sho said, "Sir, sen thou wyl wend,
Sai us thi name, so God the mend."
"Madame," he said, "bi Saint Symoun,
I hat the Knight with the Lyoun."
Sho said, "We saw yow never or now,
Ne never herd we speke of yow."
"Tharby," he sayd, "ye understand,
I am noght knawen wide in land."
Sho said, "I prai the forto dwell,
If that thou may, here us omell."
If sho had wist wele wha it was,
She wald wele lever have laten him pas;
And tharfore wald he noght be knawen
Both for hir ese and for his awyn.
He said, "No lenger dwel I ne may;
Beleves wele and haves goday.
I prai to Crist, hevyn kyng,
Lady, len yow gude lifing,
And len grace, that al yowre anoy
May turn yow unto mykel joy."
Sho said, "God grant that it so be."
Unto himself than thus said he,
"Thou ert the lok and kay also
Of al my wele and al my wo."
  Now wendes he forth and morning mase,
And nane of tham wist what he was,
Bot Lunet that he bad sold layn,

And so sho did with al hir mayne.
Sho cunvayd him forth on his way;
He said, "Gude leman, I the pray,
That thou tel to no moder son,
Who has bene thi champion;
And als I pray the, swete wight,
Late and arly thou do thi might
With speche unto my lady fre
Forto make hir frende with me.
Sen ye er now togeder glade,
Help thou that we war frendes made."
"Sertes, sir," sho sayd, "ful fayn
Thareobout wil I be bayn;
And that ye have done me this day,
God do yow mede, als he wele may."
    Of Lunet thus his leve he tase,
Bot in hert grete sorow he hase;
His lioun feled so mekill wa,
That he ne myght no ferrer ga.
Sir Ywayn puld gres in the felde
And made a kouche opon his shelde;
Thareon his lyoun laid he thare,
And forth he rides and sighes sare;
On his shelde so he him led.
Than was he ful evyl sted.
Forth he rides by frith and fell,
Til he come to a fayre castell.
Thare he cald and swith sone
The porter has the gates undone,
And to him made he ful gude chere.
He said, "Sir, ye er welcum here."
Syr Ywain said, "God do the mede,

For tharof have I mekil nede."
Yn he rade right at the gate;
Faire folk kepid hym tharate.
Thai toke his shelde and his lyoun,
And ful softly thai laid it doun;
Sum to stabil led his stede,
And sum also unlaced his wede.
   Thai talde the lord than of that knyght;
And sone he and his lady bryght
And thaire sons and doghters all
Come ful faire him forto kall;
Thai war ful fayn he thore was sted.
To chaumber sone thai have him led;
His bed was ordand richely,
And his lioun thai laid him by.
Him was no mister forto crave,
Redy he had what he wald have.
Twa maydens with him thai laft
That wele war lered of lechecraft;
The lordes doghters both thai wore
That war left to kepe hym thore.
Thai heled hym everilka wound,
And hys lyoun sone made thai sownd.
I can noght tel how lang he lay;
When he was helyd he went his way.
   Bot whils he sojorned in that place,
In that land byfel this case.
A litil thethin in a stede
A grete lord of the land was ded.
Lifand he had none other ayre
Bot two doghters that war ful fayre.
Als sone als he was laid in molde,

The elder sister sayd sho wolde
Wend to court sone als sho myght
Forto get hir som doghty knyght
Forto win hir al the land
And hald it haley in hir hand.
The yonger sister saw sho ne myght
Have that fell until hir right,
Bot if that it war by batail;
To court sho wil at ask cownsayl.
The elder sister sone was gare,
Unto the court fast gan sho fare.
To Sir Gawayn sho made hir mane,
And he has granted hyr onane,
"Bot yt bus be so prevely,
That nane wit bot thou and I.
If thou of me makes any yelp,
Lorn has thou al my help."
Than efter on the tother day
Unto kourt come the tother may,
And to Sir Gawayn sone sho went
And talde unto him hir entent;
Of his help sho him bysoght.
"Sertes," he sayd, "that may I noght."
Than sho wepe and wrang hir handes;
And right with that come new tithandes,
How a knyght with a lyoun
Had slane a geant ful feloun.
The same knight thare talde this tale
That Syr Ywayn broght fra bale
That had wedded Gawayn sister dere.
Sho and hir sons war thare infere;
Thai broght the dwergh, that be ye balde,

And to Sir Gawayn have thai talde
How the knyght with the lyowne
Delivred tham out of presowne,
And how he for Syr Gawayn sake
Gan that batayl undertake,
And als how nobilly that he wroght.
Sir Gawayn said, "I knaw him noght."
The yonger mayden than alsone
Of the king askes this bone
To have respite of fourti dais,
Als it fel to landes lays.
Sho wist thare was no man of main
That wald fyght with Sir Gawayn;
Sho thoght to seke by frith and fell
The knyght that sho herd tham of tell.
Respite was granted of this thing;
The mayden toke leve at the king
And sethen at al the baronage,
And forth sho went on hir vayage.
    Day ne nyght wald sho noght spare;
Thurgh al the land fast gan sho fare,
Thurgh castel and thurgh ilka toun
To seke the knight with the lyown:
He helpes al in word and dede,
That unto him has any nede.
Sho soght hym thurgh al that land,
Bot of hym herd sho na tythand.
Na man kouth tel hir whare he was.
Ful grete sorow in hert sho has.
So mikel murning gan sho make
That a grete sekenes gan sho take.
Bot in hir way right wele sho sped.

At that kastell was sho sted
Whare Sir Ywayn are had bene
Helid of his sekenes clene.
Thare sho was ful wele knawen
And als welcum als til hyr awyn;
With alkyn gamyn thai gan hir glade,
And mikel joy of hir thai made.
Unto the lord sho tald hyr case,
And helping hastily sho hase.

   Stil in lecheing thare sho lay;
A maiden for hir toke the way
For to seke yf that sho myght
In any land here of that knyght;
And that same kastel come sho by,
Whare Ywayn wedded the lavedy;
And fast sho spird in ylk sesown
Efter the knight with the lioun.
Thai tald hir how he went tham fra,
And also how thay saw him sla
Thre nobil knyghtes for the nanes
That faght with him al at anes.
Sho said, "Par charité, I yow pray,
If that ye wate, wil ye me say,
Whederward that he es went?"
Thai said, for soth, thai toke na tent;
"Ne here es nane that the can tell,
Bot if it be a damysell,
For whas sake he heder come,
And for hir the batayl he name.
We trow wele that sho can the wis;
Yonder in yone kyrk sho ys;
Tharfore we rede to hyr thou ga."

And hastily than did sho swa.
Aither other ful gudeli gret,
And sone she frayned at Lunet
If sho kouth ani sertan sayne.
And hendly answerd sho ogayne,
"I sal sadel my palfray
And wend with the forth on thi way
And wis the als wele als I can."
Ful oft sithes thanked sho hir than.
   Lunet was ful smertly gare,
And with the mayden forth gan sho fare.
Als thai went, al sho hyr talde,
How sho was taken and done in halde,
How wikkedly that sho was wreghed,
And how that trayturs on hir leghed,
And how that sho sold have bene brent,
Had noght God hir socore sent
Of that knight with the lyoun:
"He lesed me out of presoun."
Sho broght hir sone into a playn,
Whare sho parted fra Sir Ywayn;
Sho said, "Na mare can I tel the,
Bot here parted he fra me.
How that he went wate I no mare;
Bot wounded was he wonder-sare.
God that for us sufferd wounde.
Len us to se him hale and sownde.
No lenger with the may I dwell;
Bot cumly Crist that heried hell,
Len the grace that thou may spede
Of thine erand als thou has nede."
Lunet hastily hies hir home,

And the mayden sone to the kastel come
Whare he was helid byforehand.
The lord sone at the gate sho fand
With knyghtes and ladies grete cumpani;
Sho haylsed tham al ful hendely,
And ful fayre praied sho to tham then
If thai couth thai sold hyr ken
Whare sho myght fynd in toure or toun
A kumly knyght with a lyoun.
Than said the lord, "By swete Jhesus,
Right now parted he fra us;
Lo here the steppes of his stede,
Evyn unto him thai wil the lede."

   Than toke sho leve and went hir way,
With sporrs sho sparid noght hir palfray;
Fast sho hyed with al hyr myght,
Until sho of him had a syght
And of hys lyoun that by him ran.
Wonder joyful was sho than,
And with hir force sho hasted so fast
That sho overtoke him at the last.
Sho hailsed him with hert ful fayn,
And he hir hailsed fayre ogayn.
Sho said, "Sir, wide have I yow soght,
And for my self ne es it noght,
Bot for a damysel of pryse
That halden es both war and wise.
Men dose to hir ful grete outrage,
Thai wald hir reve hyr heritage;
And in this land now lifes none
That sho traystes hyr opone
Bot anly opon God and the,

For thou ert of so grete bounté;
Thorgh help of the sho hopes wele
To win hyr right everilka dele.
Scho sais no knyght that lifes now
Mai help hir half so wele als thou;
Gret word sal gang of thi vassage,
If that thou win hir heritage.
For thoght sho toke slike sekenes sare,
So that sho might travail no mare,
I have yow soght on sydes sere.
Tharfore yowre answer wald I here,
Whether ye wil with me wend,
Or elswhare yow likes to lend."
He said, "That knyght that idil lies
Oft sithes winnes ful litel pries.
Forthi mi rede sal sone be tane:
Gladly with the wil I gane,
Wheder so thou wil me lede,
And hertly help the in thi nede.
Sen thou haves me so wide soght,
Sertes, fail the sal I noght."

   Thus thaire wai forth gan thai hald
Until a kastel that was cald
The Castel of the Hevy Sorow.
Thare wald he bide until the morow;
Thare to habide him thoght it best,
For the son drogh fast to rest.
Bot al the men that thai with met,
Grete wonder sone on tham thai set
And said, "Thou wreche, unsely man,
Whi wil thou here thi herber tane?
Thou passes noght without despite."

Sir Ywain answerd tham als tyte
And said, "For soth, ye er unhende
An unkouth man so forto shende;
Ye sold noght say hym velany,
Bot if ye wist encheson why."
Thai answerd than and said ful sone,
"Thou sal wit or to-morn at none."
Syr Ywaine said, "For al yowre saw
Unto yon castel wil I draw."
He and his lyoun and the may
Unto the castel toke the way.
When the porter of tham had sight,
Sone he said unto the knight,
"Cumes forth," he said, "ye al togeder!
Ful ille hail er ye cumen heder."
Thus war thai welkumd at the gate,
And yit thai went al in tharate;
Unto the porter no word thai said.
A hal thai fand ful gudeli graid,
And als Sir Ywaine made entré,
Fast bisyde him than saw he
A proper place and faire, iwis,
Enclosed obout with a palis.
He loked in bitwix the trese,
And many maidens thare he sese
Wirkand silk and gold-wire;
Bot thai war al in pover atire.
Thaire clothes war reven on evil arai;
Ful tenderly al weped thai.
Thaire face war lene and als unclene,
And blak smokkes had thai on bidene;
Thai had mischefs ful manifalde

Of hunger, of threst, and of calde;
And ever onane thai weped all,
Als thai wald to water fall.
When Ywaine al this understode,
Ogayn unto the gates he gode;
Bot thai war sperred ferli fast
With lokkes that ful wele wald last.
The porter kepid tham with his main
And said, "Sir, thou most wend ogain;
I wate thou wald out at the gate,
Bot thou mai noght by na gate.
Thi herber es tane til to-morow,
And tharfore getes thou mekill sorow.
Omang thi fase here sted ertow."
He said, "So have I bene or now
And past ful wele; so sal I here.
Bot, leve frend, wiltou me lere
Of thise maidens what thai are,
That wirkes al this riche ware?"
He said, "If thou wil wit trewly,
Forthermare thou most aspy."
"Tharfore," he said, "I sal noght lett."
He soght and fand a dern weket,
He opind it and in he gede.
"Maidens," he said, "God mot yow spede,
And als He sufferd woundes sare,
He send yow covering of yowre care,
So that ye might mak merier chere."
"Sir," thai said, "God gif so were."
"Yowre sorow," he said, "unto me say,
And I sal mend it, yf I may."
Ane of tham answerd ogayne

And said, "The soth we sal noght layne;
We sal yow tel or ye ga ferr,
Why we er here and what we err.
Sir, ye sal understand
That we er al of Maydenland.
Oure kyng opon his jolité
Passed thurgh many cuntré
Aventures to spir and spy
Forto asay his owen body.
His herber here anes gan he ta;
That was biginyng of oure wa.
For heryn er twa champions;
Men sais thai er the devil sons,
Geten of a woman with a ram;
Ful many man have thai done gram.
What knight so herbers here a nyght,
With both at ones bihoves him fight.
So bus the do, by bel and boke;
Allas, that thou thine thus here toke.
Oure king was wight himself to welde
And of fourtene yeres of elde,
When he was tane with tham to fyght;
Bot unto tham had he no myght,
And when he saw him bud be ded,
Than he kouth no better rede,
Bot did him haly in thaire grace
And made tham sureté in that place,
Forto yeld tham ilka yere,
So that he sold be hale and fere,
Threty maidens to trowage,
And al sold be of hegh parage
And the fairest of his land;

Herto held he up his hand.
This ilk rent byhoves hym gyf,
Als lang als the fendes lyf,
Or til thai be in batayl tane,
Or els unto thai be al slane.
Than sal we pas al hethin quite,
That here suffers al this despite.
Bot herof es noght for speke;
Es none in werld that us mai wreke.
We wirk here silver, silk, and golde,
Es none richer on this molde,
And never the better er we kled,
And in grete hunger er we sted;
For al that we wirk in this stede,
We have noght half oure fil of brede;
For the best that sewes here any styk,
Takes bot foure penys in a wik,
And that es litel wha som tase hede,
Any of us to kleth and fede.
Ilkone of us withouten lesyng
Might win ilk wike fourty shilling;
And yit, bot if we travail mare,
Oft thai bete us wonder sare.
It helpes noght to tel this tale,
For thare bese never bote of oure bale.
Oure maste sorow, sen we bigan,
That es that we se mani a man,
Doghty dukes, yrels, and barouns,
Oft sithes slane with thir champiowns;
With tham to-morn bihoves the fight."
Sir Ywayn said, "God, maste of myght,
Sal strenkith me in ilka dede

Ogains tha devils and al thaire drede;
That lord deliver yow of yowre fase."
Thus takes he leve and forth he gase.
  He passed forth into the hall,
Thare fand he no man him to call;
No bewtese wald thai to him bede,
Bot hastily thai toke his stede
And also the maydens palfray,
War served wele with corn and hay.
For wele thai hoped that Sir Ywayn
Sold never have had his stede ogayn.
Thurgh the hal Sir Ywain gase
Intil ane orcherd playn pase;
His maiden with him ledes he.
He fand a knyght under a tre;
Opon a clath of gold he lay.
Byfor him sat a ful fayre may;
A lady sat with tham infere.
The mayden red at thai myght here,
A real romance in that place,
Bot I ne wote of wham it was.
Sho was bot fiftene yeres alde;
The knyght was lord of al that halde,
And that mayden was his ayre;
Sho was both gracious, gode, and fare.
Sone, when thai saw Sir Ywaine,
Smertly rase thai hym ogayne,
And by the hand the lord him tase,
And unto him grete myrth he mase.
He said, "Sir, by swete Jhesus,
Thou ert ful welcum until us."
The mayden was bowsom and bayne

179

Forto unarme Syr Ywayne;
Serk and breke bath sho hym broght,
That ful craftily war wroght
Of riche cloth soft als the sylk
And tharto white als any mylk.
Sho broght hym ful riche wedes to were,
Hose and shose and alkins gere.
Sho payned hir with al hir myght
To serve him and his mayden bright.
Sone thai went unto sopere,
Ful really served thai were
With metes and drinkes of the best,
And sethin war thai broght to rest.
In his chaumber by hym lay
His owin lyoun and his may.

　At morn, when it was dayes lyght,
Up thai rase and sone tham dyght.
Sir Ywayn and hys damysele
Went ful sone til a chapele,
And thare thai herd a mes in haste
That was sayd of the Haly Gaste.
Efter Mes ordand he has
Forth on his way fast forto pas;
At the lord hys leve he tase,
And grete thanking to him he mase.
The lord said, "Tak it to na greve,
To gang hethin yit getes thou na leve.
Herein es ane unsely law,
That has bene used of ald daw
And bus be done for frend or fa.
I sal do com byfor the twa
Grete serjantes of mekil myght;

And, whether it be wrang or right,
Thou most tak the shelde and spere
Ogaynes tham the forto were.
If thou overcum tham in this stoure,
Than sal thou have al this honoure
And my doghter in mariage,
And also al myne heritage."
Than said Sir Ywayn, "Als mot I the,
Thi doghter sal thou have for me;
For a king or ane emparoure
May hir wed with grete honoure."
The lord said, "Here sal cum na knyght,
That he ne sal with twa champions fight;
So sal thou do on al wise,
For it es knawen custum assise."
Sir Ywaine said, "Sen I sal so,
Than es the best that I may do
To put me baldly in thaire hend
And tak the grace that God wil send."
The champions sone war forth broght.
Sir Ywain sais, "By Him me boght,
Ye seme wele the devils sons,
For I saw never swilk champions."
Aither broght unto the place
A mikel rownd talvace
And a klub ful grete and lang,
Thik fret with mani a thwang;
On bodies armyd wele thai ware,
Bot thare hedes bath war bare.
The lioun bremly on tham blist;
When he tham saw ful wele he wist
That thai sold with his mayster fight.

He thoght to help him at his myght;
With his tayl the erth he dang,
For to fyght him thoght ful lang.
Of him a party had thai drede;
Thai said, "Syr knight, thou most nede
Do thi lioun out of this place
For to us makes he grete manace,
Or yelde the til us als creant."
He said, "That war noght mine avenant."
Thai said, "Than do thi beste oway,
And als sone sal we samyn play."
He said, "Sirs, if ye be agast,
Takes the beste and bindes him fast."
Thai said, "He sal be bun or slane,
For help of him sal thou have nane.
Thi self allane sal with us fight,
For that es custume and the right."
Than said Sir Ywain to tham sone:
"Whare wil ye that the best be done?"
"In a chamber he sal be loken
With gude lokkes ful stifly stoken."
Sir Ywain led than his lioun
Intil a chamber to presoun;
Than war bath tha devils ful balde,
When the lioun was in halde.
Sir Ywayn toke his nobil wede
And dight him yn, for he had nede;
And on his nobil stede he strade,
And baldely to tham bath he rade.
His mayden was ful sare adred,
That he was so straitly sted,
And unto God fast gan sho pray

Forto wyn him wele oway.
Than strake thai on him wonder sare
With thaire clubbes that ful strang ware;
Opon his shelde so fast thai feld
That never a pece with other held;
Wonder it es that any man
Might bere the strakes that he toke than.
Mister haved he of socoure,
For he come never in swilk a stoure;
Bot manly evyr with al his mayn
And graithly hit he tham ogayn;
And als it telles in the boke,
He gaf the dubbil of that he toke.
   Ful grete sorow the lioun has
In the chameber whare he was;
And ever he thoght opon that dede,
How he was helpid in his nede,
And he might now do na socowre
To him that helpid him in that stoure;
Might he out of the chamber breke,
Sone he walde his maister wreke.
He herd thaire strakes that war ful sterin,
And yern he waytes in ilka heryn,
And al was made ful fast to hald.
At the last he come to the thriswald;
The erth thare kest he up ful sone,
Als fast als foure men sold have done
If thai had broght bath bill and spade;
A mekil hole ful sone he made.
Yn al this was Sir Ywayn
Ful straitly parred with mekil payn,
And drede he had, als him wele aght,

For nowther of tham na woundes laght.
Kepe tham cowth thai wonder wele
That dintes derid tham never a dele;
It was na wapen that man might welde,
Might get a shever out of thaire shelde.
Tharof cowth Ywayn no rede,
Sare he douted to be ded;
And also his damysel
Ful mekil murnyng made omell,
And wele sho wend he sold be slane,
And, sertes, than war hir socore gane.
Bot fast he stighteld in that stowre,
And hastily him come socowre.
    Now es the lioun outbroken,
His maister sal ful sone be wroken.
He rynnes fast with ful fell rese,
Than helpid it noght to prai for pese!
He stirt unto that a glotowne,
And to the erth he brayd him downe.
Than was thare nane obout that place,
That thai ne war fayn of that faire chace.
The maiden had grete joy in hert;
Thai said, "He sal never rise in quert."
His felow fraisted with al his mayn
To raise him smertly up ogayn;
And right so als he stowped doun,
Sir Ywain with his brand was boun,
And strake his nek-bane right insonder,
Thareof the folk had mekil wonder.
His hevid trindeld on the sand:
Thus had Ywain the hegher hand.
When he had feld that fowl feloun,

Of his stede he lighted down.
His lioun on that other lay:
Now wil he help him, if he may.
The lioun saw his maister cum,
And to hys part he wald have som.
The right sholder oway he rase,
Both arm and klob with him he tase,
And so his maister gan he wreke.
And, als he might, yit gan he speke
And said, "Sir knight, for thi gentry,
I pray the have of me mercy;
And by scill sal he mercy have,
What man so mekely wil it crave;
And tharfore grantes mercy to me."
Sir Ywain said, "I grant it the,
If that thou wil thi selven say,
That thou ert overcumen this day."
He said, "I grant, withowten fail,
I am overcumen in this batail
For pure ataynt and recreant."
Sir Ywayn said, "Now I the grant
Forto do the na mare dere,
And fro my liown I sal the were;
I grant the pese at my powere."
   Than come the folk ful faire infere;
The lord and the lady als
Thai toke him faire obout the hals;
Thai saide, "Sir, now saltou be
Lord and syre in this cuntré,
And wed oure doghter, for sertayn."
Sir Ywain answerd than ogayn;
He said, "Sen ye gif me hir now,

I gif hir evyn ogayn to yow;
Of me forever I grant hir quite.
Bot, sir, takes it til no despite;
For, sertes, whif may I none wed,
Until my nedes be better sped.
Bot this thing, sir, I ask of the,
That al thir prisons may pas fre.
God has granted me this chance,
I have made thaire delyverance."
The lord answerd than ful tyte
And said, "I grant the tham al quite.
My doghter als, I rede, thou take;
Sho es noght worthi to forsake."
Unto the knyght Sir Ywain sais,
"Sir, I sal noght hir mysprays;
For sho es so curtays and hende,
That fra hethin to the werldes ende
Es no king ne emparoure
Ne no man of so grete honowre,
That he ne might wed that bird bright;
And so wald I, if that I myght.
I wald hir wed with ful gude chere,
Bot, lo, I have a mayden here;
To folow hir now most I nede,
Wheder so sho wil me lede.
Tharfore at this time haves goday."
He said, "Thou passes noght so oway,
Sen thou wil noght do als I tell,
In my prison sal thou dwell."
He said, "If I lay thare al my live,
I sal hir never wed to wive;
For with this maiden most I wend

Until we cum whare sho wil lend."
The lord saw it was no bote
Obout that mater more to mote.
He gaf him leve oway to fare,
Bot he had lever he had bene thare.
   Sir Ywayn takes than forth infere
Al the prisons that thare were;
Bifore hym sone thai come ilkane,
Nerehand naked and wo-bigane;
Stil he hoved at the gate,
Til thai war went al forth thareate.
Twa and twa ay went thai samyn
And made omang tham mikel gamyn.
If God had cumen fra hevyn on hight
And on this mold omang tham light,
Thai had noght made mare joy, sertain,
Than thai made to Syr Ywayne.
Folk of the toun com him biforn
And blissed the time that he was born;
Of his prowes war thai wele payd:
"In this werld es none slike," thai said.
Thai cunvayd him out of the toun
With ful faire processiowne.
The maidens than thaire leve has tane,
Ful mekil myrth thai made ilkane;
At thaire departing prayed thai thus:
"Oure lord God, mighty Jhesus,
He help yow, sir, to have yowre will
And shilde yow ever fra alkyns ill.'
"Maidens," he said, "God mot yow se
And bring yow wele whare ye wald be."
Thus thaire way forth er thai went:

Na more unto tham wil we tent.
  Sir Ywayn and his faire may
Al the sevenight traveld thai.
The maiden knew the way ful wele
Hame until that ilk castele
Whare sho left the seke may;
And theder hastily come thai.
When thai come to the castel gate,
Sho led Sir Ywain yn thareate.
The mayden was yit seke lyand;
Bot, when thai talde hir this tithand,
That cumen was hir messagere
And the knyght with hyr infere,
Swilk joy thareof sho had in hert,
Hir thoght that sho was al in quert.
Sho said, "I wate my sister will
Gif me now that falles me till."
In hir hert sho was ful light;
Ful hendly hailsed sho the knight:
"A, sir," sho said, "God do the mede,
That thou wald cum in swilk a nede."
And al that in that kastel were
Welkumd him with meri chere.
I can noght say, so God me glade,
Half the myrth that thai him made.
That night he had ful nobil rest
With alkins esment of the best.
Als sone als the day was sent,
Thai ordaind tham and forth thai went.
  Until that town fast gan thai ride
Whare the kyng sojorned that tide;
And thare the elder sister lay,

Redy forto kepe hyr day.
Sho traisted wele on Sir Gawayn,
That no knyght sold cum him ogayn;
Sho hopid thare was no knyght lifand,
In batail that might with him stand.
Al a sevenight dayes bidene
Wald noght Sir Gawayn be sene,
Bot in ane other toun he lay;
For he wald cum at the day
Als aventerous into the place,
So that no man sold se his face;
The armes he bare war noght his awyn,
For he wald noght in court be knawyn.
Syr Ywayn and his damysell
In the town toke thaire hostell;
And thare he held him prevely,
So that none sold him ascry.
Had thai dwelt langer by a day,
Than had sho lorn hir land for ay.
Sir Ywain rested thare that nyght,
And on the morn he gan hym dyght;
On slepe left thai his lyowne
And wan tham wightly out of toun.
It was hir wil and als hys awyn
At cum to court als knyght unknawyn.
  Sone obout the prime of day
Sir Gawayn fra thethin thare he lay,
Hies him fast into the felde
Wele armyd with spere and shelde;
No man knew him, les ne more,
Bot sho that he sold fight fore.
The elder sister to court come

Unto the king at ask hir dome.
Sho said, "I am cumen with my knyght
Al redy to defend my right.
This day was us set sesowne,
And I am here al redy bowne;
And sen this es the last day,
Gifes dome and lates us wend oure way.
My sister has al sydes soght,
Bot, wele I wate, here cums sho noght;
For, sertainly, sho findes nane,
That dar the batail undertane
This day for hir forto fyght
Forto reve fra me my right.
Now have I wele wonnen my land
Withowten dint of knightes hand.
What so my sister ever has mynt,
Al hir part now tel I tynt:
Al es myne to sell and gyf,
Als a wreche ay sal sho lyf.
Tharfore, Sir King, sen it es swa,
Gifes yowre dome and lat us ga."
   The king said, "Maiden, think noght lang."
(Wele he wist sho had the wrang.)
"Damysel, it es the assyse,
Whils sityng es of the justise,
The dome nedes thou most habide;
For par aventure it may bityde,
Thi sister sal cum al bi tyme,
For it es litil passed prime."
When the king had tald this scill,
Thai saw cum rideand over a hyll
The yonger sister and hir knyght;

190

The way to town thai toke ful right.
(On Ywains bed his liown lay,
And thai had stollen fra him oway.)
The elder maiden made il chere,
When thai to court cumen were.
The king withdrogh his jugement,
For wele he trowed in his entent
That the yonger sister had the right,
And that sho sold cum with sum knyght;
Himself knew hyr wele inogh.
When he hir saw, ful fast he logh;
Him liked it wele in his hert,
That he saw hir so in quert.
Into the court sho toke the way,
And to the king thus gan sho say,
"God that governs alkin thing,
The save and se, Syr Arthure the Kyng,
And al the knyghtes that langes to the,
And also al thi mery menye.
Unto yowre court, sir, have I broght
An unkouth knyght that ye knaw noght;
He sais that sothly for my sake
This batayl wil he undertake;
And he haves yit in other land
Ful felle dedes under hand;
Bot al he leves, God do him mede,
Forto help me in my nede."
Hir elder sister stode hyr by,
And tyl hyr sayd sho hastily:
"For Hys luf that lens us life,
Gif me my right withouten strife,
And lat no men tharfore be slayn."

The elder sister sayd ogayn:
"Thi right es noght, for al es myne,
And I wil have yt mawgré thine.
Tharfore, if thou preche al day,
Here sal thou no thing bere oway."
The yonger mayden to hir says,
"Sister, thou ert ful curtays,
And gret dole es it forto se,
Slike two knightes als thai be,
For us sal put thamself to spill.
Tharefore now, if it be thi will,
Of thi gude wil to me thou gif
Sumthing that I may on lif."
The elder said, "So mot I the,
Who so es ferd, I rede thai fle
Thou getes right noght, withowten fail,
Bot if thou win yt thurgh batail."
The yonger said, "Sen thou wil swa,
To the grace of God here I me ta;
And Lord als He es maste of myght,
He send his socore to that knyght
That thus in dede of charité
This day antres hys lif for me."
    The twa knightes come bifor the king
And thare was sone ful grete gedering;
For ilka man that walk might,
Hasted sone to se that syght.
Of tham this was a selly case,
That nowther wist what other wase;
Ful grete luf was bitwix tham twa,
And now er aither other fa;
Ne the king kowth tham noght knaw,

For thai wald noght thaire faces shew.
If owther of tham had other sene,
Grete luf had bene tham bitwene;
Now was this a grete selly
That trew luf and so grete envy,
Als bitwix tham twa was than,
Might bath at anes be in a man.
The knightes for thase maidens love
Aither til other kast a glove,
And wele armed with spere and shelde
Thai riden both forth to the felde;
Thai stroke thaire stedes that war kene;
Litel luf was tham bitwene.
Ful grevosly bigan that gamyn,
With stalworth speres strake thai samen.
And thai had anes togeder spoken,
Had thare bene no speres broken.
Bot in that time bitid it swa,
That aither of tham wald other sla.
Thai drow swerdes and swang obout,
To dele dyntes had thai no dout.
Thaire sheldes war shiferd and helms rifen,
Ful stalworth strakes war thare gifen.
Bath on bak and brestes thare
War bath wounded wonder sare;
In many stedes might men ken
The blode out of thaire bodies ren.
On helmes thai gaf slike strakes kene
That the riche stanes al bidene
And other gere that was ful gude,
Was overcoverd al in blode.
Thaire helmes war evel brusten bath,

And thai also war wonder wrath.
Thaire hauberkes als war al totorn
Both bihind and also byforn;
Thaire sheldes lay sheverd on the ground.
Thai rested than a litil stound
Forto tak thaire ande tham till,
And that was with thaire bother will.
Bot ful lang rested thai noght,
Til aither of tham on other soght;
A stronge stowre was tham bitwene,
Harder had men never sene.
The king and other that thare ware,
Said that thai saw never are
So nobil knightes in no place
So lang fight bot by Goddes grace.
Barons, knightes, squiers, and knaves
Said, "It es no man that haves
So mekil tresore ne nobillay,
That might tham quite thaire dede this day."
Thir wordes herd the knyghtes twa;
It made tham forto be more thra.
   Knightes went obout gude wane
To mak the two sisters at ane:
Bot the elder was so unkinde,
In hir thai might no mercy finde;
And the right that the yonger hase,
Puttes sho in the kinges grace.
The king himself and als the quene
And other knightes al bidene
And al that saw that dede that day,
Held al with the yonger may;
And to the king al thai bisoght,

Whether the elder wald or noght,
That he sold evin the landes dele
And gif the yonger damysele
The half or els sum porciowne,
That sho mai have to warisowne,
And part the two knightes intwyn.
"For, sertis," thai said, "it war grete syn,
That owther of tham sold other sla,
For in the werld es noght swilk twa.
When other knightes," said thai, "sold sese,
Thamself wald noght asent to pese."
Al that ever saw that batayl,
Of thaire might had grete mervayl.
Thai saw never under the hevyn
Twa knightes that war copled so evyn.
Of al the folk was none so wise,
That wist whether sold have the prise;
For thai saw never so stalworth stoure,
Ful dere boght thai that honowre.
Grete wonder had Sir Gawayn,
What he was that faght him ogain;
And Sir Ywain had grete ferly,
Wha stode ogayns him so stifly.
On this wise lasted that fight
Fra midmorn unto mirk night;
And by that tyme, I trow, thai twa
War ful weri and sare alswa.
Thai had bled so mekil blode,
It was grete ferly that thai stode;
So sare thai bet on bak and brest,
Until the sun was gone to rest;
For nowther of tham wald other spare.

For mirk might thai than na mare,
Tharfore to rest thai both tham yelde.
   Bot or thai past out of the felde,
Bitwix tham two might men se
Both mekil joy and grete peté.
By speche might no man Gawain knaw,
So was he hase and spak ful law;
And mekil was he out of maght
For the strakes that he had laght.
And Sir Ywain was ful wery.
Bot thus he spekes and sais in hy:
He said, "Syr, sen us failes light,
I hope it be no lifand wight,
That wil us blame if that we twin.
For of al stedes I have bene yn,
With no man yit never I met
That so wele kowth his strakes set;
So nobil strakes has thou gifen
That my sheld es al toreven."
Sir Gawayn said, "Sir, sertanly,
Thou ert noght so weri als I;
For if we langer fightand were,
I trow I might do the no dere.
Thou ert no thing in my det
Of strakes that I on the set."
Sir Ywain said, "In Cristes name,
Sai me what thou hat at hame."
He said, "Sen thou my name wil here
And covaites to wit what it were,
My name in this land mani wote;
I hat Gawayn, the King son Lote."
Than was Sir Ywayn sore agast;

196

His swerde fra him he kast.
He ferd right als he wald wede,
And sone he stirt down of his stede.
He said, "Here es a fowl mischance
For defaut of conisance.
A, sir," he said, "had I the sene,
Than had here no batel bene;
I had me yolden to the als tite,
Als worthi war for descumfite."
"What man ertou?" said Sir Gawain.
"Syr," he said, "I hat Ywayne,
That lufes the more by se and sand
Than any man that es lifand,
For mani dedes that thou me did,
And curtaysi ye have me kyd.
Tharfore, sir, now in this stoure
I sal do the this honowre:
I grant that thou has me overcumen
And by strenkyth in batayl nomen."
Sir Gawayn answerd als curtays:
"Thau sal noght do, sir, als thou sais;
This honowre sal noght be myne,
Bot, sertes, it aw wele at be thine;
I gif it the here withowten hone
And grantes that I am undone."
Sone thai light, so sais the boke,
And aither other in armes toke
And kissed so ful fele sithe;
Than war thai both glad and blithe.
In armes so thai stode togeder,
Unto the king com ridand theder;
And fast he covait forto here

Of thir knightes what thai were,
And whi thai made so mekil gamyn,
Sen thai had so foghten samyn.
  Ful hendli than asked the king,
Wha had so sone made saghteling
Bitwix tham that had bene so wrath
And aither haved done other scath.
He said, "I wend ye wald ful fain
Aither of thow have other slayn,
And now ye er so frendes dere."
"Sir King," said Gawain, "Ye sal here.
For unknawing and hard grace
Thus have we foghten in this place;
I am Gawayn, yowre awin nevow,
And Sir Ywayn faght with me now.
When we war nere weri, iwys,
Mi name he frayned and I his;
When we war knawin, sone gan we sese.
Bot, sertes, sir, this es no lese,
Had we foghten forth a stownde,
I wote wele I had gone to grounde;
By his prowes and his mayne,
I wate, for soth, I had bene slayne."
Thir wordes menged al the mode
Of Sir Ywain als he stode;
"Sir," he said, "so mot I go,
Ye knaw yowreself it es noght so.
Sir King," he said, "withowten fail,
I am overcumen in this batayl."
"Nai, sertes," said Gawain, "bot am I."
Thus nowther wald have the maistri,
Bifore the king gan aither grant,

That himself was recreant.
Than the king and hys menye
Had bath joy and grete peté;
He was ful fayn thai frendes were,
And that thai ware so funden infere.
The kyng said, "Now es wele sene
That mekil luf was yow bitwene."
He said, "Sir Ywain, welkum home!"
For it was lang sen he thare come.
He said, "I rede ye both assent
To do yow in my jujement;
And I sal mak so gude ane ende
That ye sal both be halden hende."
Thai both assented sone thartill
To do tham in the kynges will,
If the maydens wald do so.
Than the king bad knyghtes two
Wend efter the maydens bath,
And so thai did ful swith rath.

  Bifore the kyng when thai war broght
He tald unto tham als him thoght,
"Lystens me now, maydens hende,
Yowre grete debate es broght til ende;
So fer forth now es it dreven
That the dome most nedes be gifen,
And I sal deme yow als I can."
The elder sister answerd than:
"Sen ye er king that us sold were,
I pray yow do to me na dere."
He said, "I wil let for na saw
Forto do the landes law.
Thi yong sister sal have hir right,

For I se wele that thi knyght
Es overcumen in this were."
Thus said he anely hir to fere,
And for he wist hir wil ful wele,
That sho wald part with never a dele.
"Sir," sho said, "sen thus es gane,
Now most I, whether I wil or nane,
Al yowre cumandment fufill,
And tharfore dose right als ye will."
The king said, "Thus sal it fall,
Al yowre landes depart I sall.
Thi wil es wrang, that have I knawin.
Now sal thou have noght bot thin awin,
That es the half of al bydene."
Than answerd sho ful tite in tene
And said, "Me think ful grete outrage
To gif hir half myne heritage."
The king said, "For yowre bother esse
In hir land I sal hir sese,
And sho sal hald hir land of the
And to the tharfore mak fewté;
Sho sal the luf als hir lady,
And thou sal kith thi curtaysi,
Luf hir efter thine avenant,
And sho sal be to the tenant."
This land was first, I understand,
That ever was parted in Ingland.
Than said the king, "Withowten fail,
For tha luf of that batayl
Al sisters that sold efter bene
Sold part the landes tham bitwene."
    Than said the king to Sir Gawain,

And als he prayed Sir Ywain
Forto unlace thaire riche wede;
And tharto had thai bath grete nede.
Als thai thusgate stod and spak,
The lyown out of the chamber brak.
Als thai thaire armurs sold unlace,
Come he rinand to that place.
Bot he had, or he come thare,
Soght his mayster whideware;
And ful mekil joy he made
When he his mayster funden hade.
On ilka side than might men se,
The folk fast to toun gan fle;
So war thai ferd for the liowne
Whan thai saw him theder bown.
Syr Ywain bad tham cum ogayn
And said, "Lordinges, for sertayn,
Fra this beste I sal yow were,
So that he sal do yow no dere.
And, sirs, ye sal wele trow mi sawes;
We er frendes and gude felaws.
He es mine and I am his;
For na tresore I wald him mys."
   When thai saw this was sertain,
Than spak thai al of Sir Ywaine:
"This es the Knight with the Liown,
That es halden of so grete renown.
This ilk knight the geant slogh;
Of dedis he es doghty inogh."
Than said Sir Gawayn sone in hi,
"Me es bitid grete velani;
I cri the mercy, Sir Ywayne,

That I have trispast the ogayn.
Thou helped mi syster in hir nede;
Evil have I quit the now thi mede.
Thou anterd thi life for luf of me;
And als mi sister tald of the,
Thou said that we ful fele dawes
Had bene frendes and gude felawes.
Bot wha it was ne wist I noght.
Sethen have I had ful mekil thoght,
And yit for al that I do can,
I cowth never here of na man,
That me coth tell toure ne town
Of the Knight with the Liown."
When thai had unlaced thaire wede,
Al the folk toke ful gode hede,
How that beste his bales to bete
Likked his maister both hend and fete.
Al the men grete mervail hade
Of the mirth the lyown made.
When the knightes war broght to rest,
The king gert cum sone of the best
Surgiens that ever war sene
Forto hele tham both bidene.

   Sone so thai war hale and sownd,
Sir Ywayn hies him fast to found.
Luf was so in his hert fest,
Night ne day haved he no rest,
Bot he get grace of his lady,
He most go wode or for luf dy.
Ful preveli forth gan he wende
Out of the court fra ilka frende.
He rides right unto the well,

And thare he thinkes forto dwell.
His gode lyon went with him ay,
He wald noght part fro him oway.
He kest water opon the stane:
The storm rase ful sone onane,
The thoner grisely gan outbrest;
Him thoght als al the grete forest
And al that was obout the well
Sold have sonken into hell.
   The lady was in mekyl dout,
For al the kastel walles obout
Quoke so fast that men might think
That al into the erth sold synk.
Thai trembled fast, both boure and hall,
Als thai unto the grund sold fall.
Was never in this mydlerde
In no kastell folk so ferde.
Bot wha it was wele wist Lunet;
Sho said, "Now er we hard byset;
Madame, I ne wate what us es best,
For here now may we have no rest.
Ful wele I wate ye have no knight,
That dar wende to yowre wel and fight
With him that cumes yow to asaile;
And, if he have here no batayle
Ne findes none yow to defend,
Yowre lose bese lorn withouten end."
The lady said sho wald be dede;
"Dere Lunet, what es thi rede?
Wirk I wil by thi kounsail,
For I ne wate noght what mai avail."
"Madame," sho said, "I wald ful fayn

Kownsail yow if it might gayn.
Bot in this case it war mystere
To have a wiser kownsaylere."
And by desait than gan sho say,
"Madame, par chance this ilk day
Sum of yowre knightes mai cum hame
And yow defend of al this shame."
"A," sho said, "Lunet, lat be;
Speke namore of my menye;
For wele I wate, so God me mend,
I have na knight me mai defend.
Tharfore my kownsail bus the be,
And I wil wirk al efter the,
And tharfore help at al thi myght."
"Madame," sho said, "had we that knyght,
That es so curtais and avenant
And has slane the grete geant,
And als that the thre knightes slogh,
Of him ye myght be trist inogh.
Bot forthermar, madame, I wate,
He and his lady er at debate
And has bene so ful many day;
And als I herd hym selvyn say,
He wald bileve with no lady
Bot on this kownand utterly,
That thai wald mak sertayn ath
To do thaire might and kunyng bath
Trewly both by day and naght
To mak him and hys lady saght."
 The lady answerd sone hir tyll,
"That wil I do with ful gode will;
Unto the here mi trowth I plight

That I sal tharto do mi might."
Sho said, "Madame, be ye noght wrath,
I most nedes have of yow an ath,
So that I mai be sertayn."
The lady said, "That will I fayn."
Lunet than riche relikes toke,
The chalis and the mes-boke;
On knese the lady down hir set
(Wit ye wele, than liked Lunet),
Hir hand opon the boke sho laid,
And Lunet althus to hir said,
"Madame," sho said, "Thou salt swere here
That thou sal do thi powere
Both dai and night opon al wise
Withouten anikyns fayntise
To saghtel the Knyght with the Liown
And his lady of grete renowne,
So that no faut be funden in the."
Sho said, "I grant, it sal so be."
Than was Lunet wele paid of this;
The boke sho gert hir lady kys.
    Sone a palfray sho bistrade,
And on hir way fast forth sho rade.
The next way ful sone sho nome,
Until sho to the well come.
Sir Ywain sat under the thorn,
And his lyoun lay him byforn.
Sho knew him wele by his lioun,
And hastily sho lighted downe;
And als sone als he Lunet sagh,
In his hert than list him lagh.
Mekil mirth was when thai met,

Aither other ful faire has gret.
Sho said, "I love grete God in trone
That I have yow fun so sone,
And tithandes tel I yow biforn;
Other sal my lady be manesworn
On relikes and bi bokes brade,
Or els ye twa er frendes made."
Sir Ywain than was wonder glad
For the tithandes that he had;
He thanked hir ful fele sith
That sho wald him slike gudenes kith,
And sho him thanked mekill mare
For the dedes that war done are.
So ather was in other det,
That both thaire travail was wele set.
He sais, "Talde thou hir oght my name?"
Sho said, "Nay, than war I to blame.
Thi name sho sal noght wit for me,
Til ye have kyssed and saghteld be."
   Than rade thai forth toward the town,
And with tham ran the gude lyoun.
When thai come to the castel gate,
Al went thai in thareat.
Thai spak na word to na man born
Of al the folk thai fand byforn.
Als sone so the lady herd sayn,
Hir damisel was cumen ogayn
And als the liown and the knight,
Than in hert sho was ful lyght;
Scho covait ever of al thing
Of him to have knawlageing.
Sir Ywain sone on knese him set,

When he with the lady met.
Lunet said to the lady sone,
"Take up the knight, madame, have done!
And, als covenand bituix us was,
Makes his pese fast or he pas."
Than did the ladi him up rise;
"Sir," sho said, "opon al wise,
I wil me pain in al thing
Forto mak thi saghtelyng
Bitwix the and thi lady bryght."
"Medame," said Lunet, "That es right,
For nane bot ye has that powere.
Al the soth now sal ye here.
Madame," sho said, "es noght at layn,
This es my lord Sir Ywaine.
Swilk luf God bitwix yow send,
That may last to yowre lives end."
   Than went the lady fer obak,
And lang sho stode or that sho spak.
Sho said, "How es this, damysele?
I wend thou sold be to me lele,
That makes me, whether I wil or noght,
Luf tham that me wa has wroght,
So that me bus be forsworn
Or luf tham that wald I war lorn.
Bot, whether it torn to wele or ill,
That I have said, I sal fulfill."
Wit ye wele, than Sir Ywaine
Of the wordes was ful fayne.
"Madame," he said, "I have miswroght,
And that I have ful dere boght.
Grete foly I did, the soth to say,

When that I past my terme-day;
And, sertes, wha so had so bityd,
Thai sold have done right als I dyd.
Bot I sal never thorgh Goddes grace
At mi might do more trispase;
And what man so wil mercy crave,
By Goddes law he sal it have."
Than sho asented saghteling to mak;
And sone in arms he gan hir tak
And kissed hir ful oft sith:
Was he never are so blith.

   Now has Sir Ywain ending made
Of al the sorows that he hade.
Ful lely lufed he ever hys whyfe
And sho him als hyr owin life;
That lasted to thaire lives ende.
And trew Lunet, the maiden hende,
Was honord ever with ald and ying
And lifed at hir owin likyng.
Of alkins thing sho has maystri,
Next the lord and the lady.
Al honord hir in toure and toun.
Thus the Knyght with the Liown
Es turned now to Syr Ywayn
And has his lordship al ogayn;
And so Sir Ywain and his wive
In joy and blis thai led thaire live.
So did Lunet and the liown
Until that ded haves dreven tham down.

   Of tham na mare have I herd tell
Nowther in rumance ne in spell.
Bot Jhesu Criste for his grete grace

In hevyn-blis grante us a place
To bide in, if his wills be.
Amen, amen, par charité.

Ywain and Gawayn thus makes endyng
God grant us all hys dere blyssing.
   Amen.